T0245503

COURTSHIP
OF THE
SAINTS

COURTSHIP
OF THE
SAINTS

How the Saints Met Their Spouses

Patrick O'Hearn

TAN Books

Gastonia, North Carolina

Cover design by Caroline Green

Cover image: The Meeting of Joachim and Anne outside the Golden Gate of Jerusalem, Filippino Lippi, 1497. Public domain via Wikimedia Commons.

Library of Congress Control Number: 2023930218

ISBN: 978-1-5051-3006-5
Kindle ISBN: 978-1-5051-3007-2
ePUB ISBN: 978-1-5051-3008-9

Published in the United States by
TAN Books
PO Box 269
Gastonia, NC 28053
www.TANBooks.com

Printed in India

This book is lovingly dedicated to Our Lady, the spouse of the Holy Spirit, and to my wife, Amanda.

"We are born to love, we live to love, and we will die to love still more."[1]

—Saint Joseph Cafasso

[1] "Saints of the Day-Joseph Cafasso," CatholicSaints.Info, catholic saints.info/saints-of-the-day-joseph-cafasso/.

CONTENTS

PART II: COURTSHIP COUNSEL AND PRAYERS

CONTENTS

PREFACE

OF ALL THE moments in our short lives, the firsts are what we remember: our first gazing upon the ocean, making our First Holy Communion, holding our child for the first time. For those of us called to marriage, one of the most memorable moments is when we first met our spouse. You can recall it vividly. Perhaps your heart started racing and your palms got sweaty. It was a sacred moment, a moment when heaven touched earth, when God intervened in time and space. Some of us may have experienced love at first sight, while others fell in love over time. Meeting our spouse takes our soul back to the greatest proposal of all time, the time when God sent the archangel Gabriel to propose to Mary on His behalf. By her *fiat*, Mary became the spouse of the Holy Spirit. But before the archangel Gabriel proposed to Mary, she received another proposal—from Saint Joseph. Mary is, in fact, the only person in the world to be proposed to by both man and angel.

When I first met my wife Amanda in graduate school, I experienced an indefinable sense of something sacred. Although I presume I did not have an archangel present at my side like Mary did, I now believe my guardian angel and my wife's joined forces that day. I didn't think, *I am going to marry this girl!*, but there was something different about her that escaped me at the time. Today, I believe it was the Holy Spirit, a spirit of peace that overcame me and took over my life. And it was a moment that almost never could have happened, save for the word of this same Spirit.

Two years after I obtained my undergraduate degree, I joined a Benedictine monastery for nearly three years. At the start of my novitiate, my abbot chose my new religious name—Raphael—after Saint Raphael. Perhaps this was not a coincidence, as Saint Raphael is the patron of those finding a spouse. At one point, a grandmother asked me to pray to Saint Raphael that her granddaughter would meet a holy spouse. She was concerned because her granddaughter was in her thirties and her prospects seemed slim. And so I sought Saint Raphael's intercession every night for a year, asking that he would help this woman find a spouse. A year later, the grandmother told me her granddaughter was engaged, and I became even more convinced that God and His saints truly wish to bring about holy marriages.

It was only recently that Pope Benedict XVI learned how his parents met, which will be recounted in this book along with several other beautiful marriage stories. At some point, every couple ought to write down how they met their spouse and share it with their children and grandchildren someday to inspire in them the confidence that true love is worth the wait.

How I wish I could have read about my grandparents' love story. Sadly, many devout couples, now deceased, have had children and grandchildren who strayed from the Faith, and who are now living in sinful relationships and miserable marriages. Perhaps if their children and grandchildren could have read about their sacrifices to keep the Faith and to remain pure, they might have followed their ancestors' holy example.

We live in times when marriage is under diabolical attack. In today's age young men do not know how to pursue a woman chastely and purely because their parents and the culture have failed to show them how. Nowadays a young woman will give herself away to get love, only to be used and hurt. We live in times when more people are cohabitating and postponing marriage than ever before. As a result, young men and women wonder if there is such a thing as true love and whether it is worth fighting for. But there is a remedy for all this, and it is called courtship.

ACKNOWLEDGMENTS

I WOULD LIKE to express my deepest gratitude to those who helped make this book possible by their support, prayers, and proofreads:

Dr. Germain and Ortrud Bianchi, Charles Coulombe, Kevin Hogan, Mattia Iannello, Monika Jablonska, Roxanne Lum, Fr. Chad Ripperger, Dr. Enrico Solinas, Michael and Heather Vento, Luke Zemlick.

In a special way, I would like to thank Gianna Emanuela Molla, the daughter of saintly parents, for helping me convey her parents' love story with accuracy and truth.

I would like to thank my publisher, TAN Books, especially Mr. Bob Gallagher, Conor Gallagher, and my editor, Brian Kennelly. There are so many more unsung heroes at TAN that would fill up this entire page. And I would like to thank my late predecessor, John Moorehouse. I never met you, but I have felt your intercession. I would like to thank Deacon Thomas and Heather Martin for reflecting what a holy marriage should look like. I would like to thank all the holy priests who helped prepare me for marriage, especially Father Lester Knoll, OFM Cap, and Monsignor John Williams.

I would like to thank my parents, Steve and Maureen, for their deep faith and their love for each other, along with my brothers, Brian and Jeff, and their wives, Erin and

Colleen. In a special way, I would like to thank my wife, Amanda, the true love of my life. This book would not be possible without you.

Finally, I would like to thank God and these saintly couples presented in this book. May all who read this book love with their same passion!

INTRODUCTION

THE ESSENCE OF our existence both now and for all eternity is to fall in love. With each passing day, we ought to love and suffer for God more than the previous day. Should we reach heaven, God willing, we will never exhaust our love for God and God's love for us. Our union will be ever new as we seek to behold the Beatific Vision throughout eternity while God unveils such mysteries too profound for the human mind to grasp. Each moment and each new insight into God's unfathomable mercy shall make us only love and praise Him all the more.

On earth, human love ought to mirror the Divine Love: the eternal exchange of love between the Father, the Son, and the Holy Spirit. Only those couples who seek to resemble the Trinitarian love and Christ's love for His Church by holding nothing back from their spouses all the days of their life can obtain the perfection of love. Couples who madly love and sacrifice for each other lead their children to heaven. These couples become living icons of the Blessed Trinity. And their children cannot help being drawn into the Divine Love when they experience their parents' unconditional love for them, or when they see their parents lay down their lives for one another. A child who sees his father gaze into his mother's eyes or his mother gladly serving his father is given a glimpse into eternity.

Long before every married couple met, it was God who peered into the future. He saw every child who was to be conceived and every marriage that ought to be. It was God who put the desire for marriage in many hearts, and it was God who created us not only for Himself but, in a mysterious way, for our spouse, intending us to be the perfect helpmate just like Eve was created for Adam. It should come as no surprise, then, that when we met (or will meet) our spouse for the first time, there was a lot of "pre-planning" that went into this moment (as in, planning from all eternity!). I imagine God smiling when He hears our hearts saying, "Wow. This person is perfect for me. I want to spend the rest of my life with her." God, who created the world out of nothing, knows what He is about. His designs are perfect even though at times we don't see them amidst our fallen world; they are perfect in spite of our sinfulness. Yes, God wills that His children experience marriage the way He intended it to be: one of joy and one of sacrificial love as we traverse this valley of tears to eternity.

Many people have entered marriage blindly. They "fall in love" based solely on physical attraction, social status, and material wealth, while overlooking virtue, the most fundamental quality. They would have been much happier had they put virtue over the externals.

At many weddings today, God is not even invited to the celebration. Beaches and scenic gardens have replaced God's holy house. Many of us blindly enter marriage only thinking about what we can receive instead of what we can offer. We have accepted the false notion of emotional love instead of true sacrificial love seen most visibly on the cross. When we do the former, we are walking into a minefield and we fail to turn to God, the only Person who can make our marriage what it is meant to be.

Some cultures offer an alternative to the current plight of divorce. For instance, in some cultures, the bride walks down the aisle with a crucifix in her hands and not a bouquet. And before the couple exchanges their kiss on the altar, they first kiss the cross, because the cross is the only remedy to the alarming statistic that nearly half of all Christian marriages end in divorce. Sadly, as more people cohabitate and enter into same-sex relationships, not to mention nearly a fourth of our generation being aborted, many devout, single people will sometimes ask the question: *Will I ever meet the person God intended me to marry?*

As a disclaimer, this book does not promise that if you pray a novena or imitate these saints presented here that God will help you meet the person of your dreams. Truth be told, God owes us nothing. Isn't God's grace and love enough? Is not seeing God face to face in heaven greater than any experience on earth, including falling in love with another person? This book sheds light on the reality that many in the Church forget—that marriage is a vocation.

In every vocation, we are expected to carry the cross that will lead us to heaven. When we idealize the notion of some perfect person whom God will send us, it's helpful to recall the words of J. R. R. Tolkien to his son: "When the glamour wears off, or merely works a bit thin, they think they have made a mistake, and that the real soul-mate is still to find. The real soul-mate too often proves to be the next sexually attractive person that comes along."[1] Tolkien believed that finding one's soulmate was at the "root" cause of the divorce culture. To overcome the endless quest to find that "one person," Tolkien argued that "the 'real soulmate' is the one you are actually married to. You really do very little choosing: life and circumstance do most of it (though if there is a God these must be His instruments, or His appearances)."[2]

The average seminarian spends at least eight years in preparation before becoming a priest, a religious brother at least four before final vows, and religious sisters at least ten before final vows. On the other hand, many couples spend less than two years together before getting married. But in all truthfulness, God has been preparing them for the sacrament of Matrimony since birth. For many, it began with their parents' beautiful witness of sacrificial love, even their parents' hidden prayers for their future spouse from their infancy. It began with other devout married people who planted seeds through their openness to life and love for each other and their children.

God expects much of those called to marriage. Specifically, every parent has a solemn duty to prepare their children for their future vocations: "It is imperative to give suitable and timely instruction to young people, above all in the heart of their own families, about the dignity of married love, its role and its exercise, so that, having learned the value of chastity, they will be able at a suitable age to

---

[1] Tolkien, *The Letters of J. R. R. Tolkien,* 51.
[2] Tolkien, 51.

engage in honorable courtship and enter upon a marriage of their own."[3]

The stories you are about to read are better than any romantic novel because they return to the source of love: God Himself. Our Lord was clear when He said, "For where there are two or three gathered together in my name, there am I in the midst of them" (Matt. 18:20). When couples, especially the saints, meet each other for the first time, God is there. He is the divine gaze behind their gaze, He is the divine touch behind their touch, and He is the breath behind their kiss. From Adam and Eve to the lives of the saints, God rejoices in holy marriages between His sons and daughters. What architect does not delight in his finished masterpiece? Yes, God invented marriage when He created mankind in His own image as "male and female" (Gen. 1:27).

Despite the circumstances surrounding the meetings of these saints and their courtship, whether it was arranged or was love at first sight,[4] it was God Himself who orchestrated everything, for He had their spouses in His mind when He created them. It is important to note that the stories you are about to read do not include all the stages of courtship, which will be discussed in the next chapter.

Our culture will only be renewed when the family is strong, that is, when marriages reflect Christ's radical

---

[3] CCC 1632, quoting *Gaudium et spes*.

[4] J. R. R. Tolkien said to his son about love at first sight, "Often love at first sight, we catch a vision, I suppose, of marriage as it should have been in an unfallen world. In this fallen world we have as our only guides, prudence, wisdom (rare in youth, too late in age), a clean heart, and fidelity of will." Tolkien, *The Letters of J.R.R. Tolkien*, 52.

love for His Church; when couples love each other madly through the good times and the bad, and are open to the number of children God wants to provide them. And this begins when people learn from the best—the saints—how true love can be found and lived out. In the words of Saint Joseph Cafasso, "we are born to love," but even more so, we are born to love madly like Christ, now and for all eternity. The quest for true love can only be found when we pursue our spouse as Christ pursues us.

Some marriage stories are naturally more inspiring, miraculous, or romantic than others, yet the common theme in all these stories is how God intervened in a real way. At every Mass, heaven intervenes in a miraculous way when Jesus becomes truly present on the altar. Sadly, this greatest of miracles is often downplayed because we grow accustomed to it. Similarly, many people can trivialize the beauty of a man and woman falling in love because it, too, seems so commonplace. Yet, despite its seemingly ordinary nature, marriage is truly extraordinary because at the right moment God intervenes and brings two people together, people whose lives will impact generation upon generation—spanning into eternity.

PART I

SAINTLY ENCOUNTERS

CHAPTER 1

COURTSHIP DEFINED

"Since marriage is beautifully sacred, so should be the courtship that precedes it. Your courtship must be pure if it is to be happy; and pure and happy, it will provide the test of character that is necessary for a blessed and a happy marriage. Only too frequently an improper courtship results in an unhappy marriage."[5]

—Father Lawrence G. Lovasik, SVD

THE WORD "COURTSHIP" carries a sense of mystery and valor, such as a knight clad in armor rescuing a distressed maiden from her looming, unhappy, arranged marriage. Not surprisingly, courtship hearkens back to the medieval era. The term, introduced in the 1570s, meant "behavior of a courtier," from the words "court" and "ship." A courtier was a person who attended the court as an adviser to the king or queen. During the sixteenth century, courtship was referred to as "the wooing of a woman, attention paid by a man to a woman with the intention of winning her affection and ultimately her consent to marriage."[6]

---

[5] Lovasik, *Clean Love in Courtship*, 1–2.
[6] "Courtship," Online Etymology Dictionary, etymonline.com/word /courtship.

In 1830, courtship was described as a time when couples developed a romantic relationship with marriage as the end goal. In other words, courtship is a means to an end. From a Catholic perspective, courtship is a period of serious discernment when a man and a woman determine whether to enter the sacrament of Matrimony together.

The question of how long a courtship should last will be discussed in detail below; for now let us consider some great general advice on this issue from Father Lawrence G. Lovasik, SVD: "While the Church warns against courtships of undue brevity, *she likewise counsels against those of excessive length*. No hard and fast rule can be laid down determining the exact length of courtship. It should be of sufficient duration to allow young people to learn the character and disposition of each other quite well."[7]

At the heart of courtship lies a discernment of the other's virtue or lack thereof. It is a litmus test of sorts. Whether the person is attractive or has a lot of money is not a reason for choosing to marry someone. Unfortunately, these are the primary reasons many do marry, and they are some of the many reasons why divorce is so prevalent.

Since many readers of this book are discerning marriage, the following quote from the Venerable Fulton Sheen is too rich to omit. He declared,

> Beauty in a woman and strength in a man are two of the most evident spurs to love. Physical beauty and vitality increase vigor in each other, but it is to be noticed that beauty in a woman and strength in a

---

[7]   Lovasik, *Clean Love in Courtship*, 61.

man are given by God to serve purposes of allure-
ment. They come at that age of life when men and
women are urged to marry one another. They are
not permanent possessions. They are something like
frosting on a cake, or like the electric starter of an
automobile motor. If love were based only on the
fact that she is a model and he is a fullback on the
football team, marriage would never endure. But
just as frosting on the cake leads to the cake itself, so
too do these allurements pass on to greater treasures.

Once on congratulating a wife who had a very
handsome husband we heard her reply: "I no longer
notice that he is handsome; I notice now that he has
greater qualities."[8]

The greater qualities, the virtues, are the magnets that
draw holy couples to each other and keep them bound for
life with God's grace. When the body breaks down, love
remains. At the same time, one ought to be attracted to
their spouse. But attraction, like the "bells and smells" at
Holy Mass, ought to lead one deeper into the heart of the
person, just as those qualities of the Mass lead one deeper
into the Eucharistic Heart of Christ.

Courtship looks to the future—to eternity. Courtship
asks the following questions: Does this person have virtue? Is this the best person to lead me—and, God willing,
my future children—to heaven? Does this person have
what it takes spiritually, emotionally, and financially?
Specifically, does he attend Mass every Sunday? Does he

---

[8] Sheen, *Fulton J. Sheen's Guide to Contentment*, 15.

pray daily? Does he go to confession regularly? Does he avoid mortal sin? Does he have a good relationship with his family?[9] Ultimately, does this person desire to become a saint with me?

Dating, on the other hand, focuses mostly on the present and forgets the ultimate purpose of meeting someone special: to enter into a holy marriage. Because some people use dating and courtship interchangeably, the lines have become blurred. According to author Beth Bailey, "the first recorded uses of the word *date* in modern meaning are from lower-class slang," by way of Chicago author George Ade in 1896.[10] During the beginning of the twentieth century, dating referred to lower-class men and women going out in public.[11] In the years leading up to World War II, dating had nothing to do with sex or marriage, but was more of a measure of one's popularity.[12] Today, our over-sexualized world has made it worse. When asking a woman out, many men are only concerned with that night and how far they can go. A person interested in dating typically has no real desire to preserve virginity or grow in virtue because the moment is all that counts.[13] There are

---

[9] A more complete checklist, almost like an examination of conscience to find the right spouse, can be found at the back of this book. It is called, "How to Choose Your Spouse."

[10] Bailey, *From Front Porch to Back Seat: Courtship in Twentieth-Century America*, 17.

[11] Bailey, *From Front Porch to Back Seat*, 17.

[12] Bailey, 26.

[13] For these reasons, courtship is recommended over dating, though the latter can also be holy, provided it is chaste and never loses sight of the end goal of marriage. Not every person will go through the four stages of courtship that will be spelled out shortly. In fact, as fewer

no fast rules for dating, while courtship involves a more formal process.

Because dating is less "formal" than courtship, it seems more concerned with the externals: Where did he go to college? What is his profession? What type of car does he drive? How physically fit is he? Does he share my interests? Is he a Democrat or a Republican? This is the secular world's checklist for finding a future spouse. Little is said about God or virtue.

On the other hand, the Catholic Church and her shepherds like Venerable Fulton Sheen have stressed the beauty of chastity and purity when it comes to marriage preparation. Most notably, Sheen highlights four phases of life: togetherness, separation, crystallization, and courtship.[14]

Togetherness involves the innocence of two children playing together. This phase occurs when children are very young. During the separation stage, boys and girls distance themselves from each other, allowing them to develop their proper psychological and physical qualities. In crystallization, they bestow upon each other various

---

people are getting married, dating can be a holy way that leads to marriage if God and His commands are the focal point of the two people's lives. This type of dating resembles more "friendship dating," listed under the first stage of courtship and mentioned in the later section, "For Those Discerning Marriage." It is a period of getting to know someone without any signs of affection or expectations. Whether a man ultimately pursues a woman through these four stages of courtship, God calls him to pursue a lady with virtue, especially chastity and purity. And the same for the woman: she too must seek someone who practices chastity and purity.

[14] Fulton J. Sheen, "Courtship," The Catholic World, June 24, 2014, https://www.youtube.com/watch?v=X3QTbVxO6kA.

positive qualities. They begin to adore one another. They begin to desire infinite happiness, but they err by "placing the infinite in the finite," looking on each other as "gods" or "angels."[15] They are interested in the opposite sex but are chiefly concerned with their physical appearance. They become "experts" of love, and they consider their parents ignorant of it.

During courtship, Sheen mentions the notion of affinity—an interest in the opposite sex that goes beyond physical attraction. Sheen declares, "The real test is . . . if they can share not only the joys of life, but also the frustrations."[16] This is the first condition. Then comes the test of sacrifice. If the man is selfish before marriage, then he will likely continue so. That is why a woman should look for a spirit of sacrifice in her future spouse, according to Sheen. When discerning his spouse, the man should ask: "Has she femininity? . . . Every woman was made to be a mother: either physically or spiritually."[17] Sheen challenges the man to look for "depth" that transcends beauty. Is she able to pass along her virtues, her Faith, and her knowledge to her children? "The more a woman is holy, the more she is a woman."[18] If the couple prays together, they will be of one heart and of one mind.

Father Chad Ripperger also defines four stages of courtship, though his stages differ somewhat from those of Bishop Sheen.[19] According to Father Ripperger, the

[15] Sheen, "Courtship."
[16] Sheen, "Courtship."
[17] Sheen, "Courtship."
[18] Sheen, "Courtship."
[19] Chad Ripperger, "Four Stages of Courtship," Sensus Fidelium.

four stages of courtship include: friendship, courtship, betrothal/engagement, and marriage.[20] These stages are more widely known today in traditional circles compared to Sheen's stages. Throughout the courtship process, a father must protect his daughter's honor.[21] He becomes the gatekeeper and watchman over his daughter's soul. And his daughter's soul is far more precious than any material possession he seeks to protect. His primary duty then is to make sure the potential suitor is "honorable."[22] A father's primary question then becomes, "Will he (the potential suitor) actually help my daughter save her soul?"[23]

The friendship stage of courtship lasts around three to six months, though this time can vary. No affection occurs during this stage in order to maintain the couple's "clarity of judgment."[24] The most important thing is whether the person has adequate virtue. One indication of virtue is if they can avoid affection during this stage and the next. Virtue will endure, not good looks, love at first sight, or even the greatest chemistry. Discovering virtue in the other person occurs in all of the stages of the courtship, because what you see now in your potential spouse is what

---

August 5, 2016, youtube.com/watch?v=r1V4w38v2mI. Note: These four stages are based on a variety of sources including Saint Thomas Aquinas's writings as well as Catholic cultures prior to the twentieth century. These four stages are also based on basic human psychology and how certain things affect people.

[20] Ripperger, "Four Stages of Courtship."
[21] Ripperger, "Four Stages of Courtship."
[22] Ripperger, "Four Stages of Courtship."
[23] Ripperger, "Four Stages of Courtship."
[24] Ripperger, "Four Stages of Courtship."

you will see later in life. Good habits and bad habits do not disappear easily.

Besides identifying virtue in the man, the woman ought to see if he can financially support her. And just because both couples have virtue does not necessarily mean that you must move to the next stage. Perhaps there is little chemistry, little attraction, or a dislike of the other's temperament. These factors must be considered along with promptings from the Holy Spirit.

Near the end of the friendship stage, the man and woman should observe the other's relationship with their family. The way a person treats his or her parents will likely be the way they treat their spouse. When you marry someone, you also marry into his or her family. The problems and generational sins of his family, but especially those he grapples with, could likely impact your marriage.[25] Marriage requires a great deal of virtue and supernatural grace to combat the rise of divorce and secular influences.

After the friendship stage comes courtship, initiating exclusivity.[26] A man ought to ask permission from the father to court his daughter. Like the friendship stage, courtship lasts around three to six months. Furthermore, the couple continues to avoid being alone together

---

[25] One must pay attention to the various impediments to marriage. Some priests have argued that if any man is struggling with pornography, he should not be courting a girl. Some will also argue that if there is significant debt, this is an impediment. These are things to discuss with a holy priest. A wounded person should seek adequate healing before pursuing someone or being pursued.

[26] Ripperger, "Four Stages of Courtship."

and shows no affection, a counter-cultural witness that seems extreme in our time. However, Father Ripperger reminds us that affection creates bonding and, therefore, terminating a relationship after sharing physical affection would result in hurt and regret—a sin of injustice. That is why bonding is meant for the permanence found only in marriage.[27] So much emotional damage could be avoided if affection were saved for the betrothal and marriage stages.

Herein lies the wisdom of courtship over dating. Avoiding affection before its proper time will cultivate and defend virtue at all costs, or, as Saint Thomas Aquinas declared, "For a person is properly called our friend when we want some good thing for him."[28] To love someone is to will the best for him or her. But to will the best for them, to truly love them, means that person will be better off by not showing affection before betrothal in case the relationship should unexpectedly end. Yes, there might be some level of disappointment, but you have made each other holier, for love triumphed over lust.

In the courtship stage, the man must look primarily to see if the woman will "submit to his lead" while the woman looks to see if the man will deny himself and sacrifice for her.[29] Self-denial is at the heart of this stage.[30] And if this virtue is evident, then the couple ought to proceed to the next stage.

---

[27] Ripperger, "Four Stages of Courtship."
[28] ST I-II 26, 4 ad 1.
[29] Ripperger, "Four Stages of Courtship."
[30] Ripperger, "Four Stages of Courtship."

Following courtship comes the betrothal/engagement stage when the man asks the father for permission to marry his daughter. Keep in mind that the father has the authority to end the courtship at any time or refuse his daughter's hand in marriage, though most men today likely wouldn't submit to this.[31] If the father agrees to the proposal and his daughter says "yes," the couple still cannot show any affection until the formal betrothal, the mutual promise of marriage.

There is a liturgical Rite of Betrothal[32] that takes place at a church along with a priest and two witnesses, accompanied by beautiful prayers and blessings. The Rite of Betrothal has been passed down to us by our Jewish elders. In this rite, the couple promises in the name of the Lord to take their future spouse in holy Matrimony. The priest also takes the two ends of his stole and, in the form of a cross, places them over the couple's hands, witnessing their "formal" proposal to marry. The man will then place the engagement ring on his fiancée's finger and the priest will bless it.

After the betrothal, the couple can engage in some levels of affection.[33] By the formal betrothal, a couple is now bound to marry except for serious reasons. To prevent scandal, the engaged/betrothed couple should not be alone together. A man must protect other people's

---

[31] Ripperger, "Four Stages of Courtship."

[32] For more information on this topic see Gregory DiPippo's article, "A Liturgical Rite of Betrothal," New Liturgical Movement, www.newliturgicalmovement.org/2019/10/a-liturgical-rite-of-betrothal.html#.Xbhzf0ZKi70.

[33] Ripperger, "Four Stages of Courtship."

views of his future spouse.[34] The woman begins to follow the man's lead. Hence the betrothal period is a time for a couple to intensify their prayer life as they prepare for marriage.

Like the friendship and courtship stages, the betrothal/ engagement stage lasts between three to six months depending on the diocese.[35] The principal action is for the couple to grow in the virtue of moderation.[36] The couple spends more time together than in the previous stages, in order to develop their virtues together. The couple must work to avoid anything that could violate the sixth and ninth commandments.[37]

Marriage is the final stage of courtship. God does not want you to have a good marriage. No, God wants you to have a holy and blessed marriage! God wants you to experience heaven now through your vows, though at times you may experience suffering to further detach you from this life. Above all, God wants you to marry the person who will help you carry your cross joyfully. Men, God wants you to be Saint Joseph for your spouse. And women, God wants you to be Mary for your husband.

---

[34] Ripperger, "Four Stages of Courtship."
[35] Father Ripperger argues that the length of the courtship process (from the first meeting to the wedding day) should be between nine months and eighteen months. Others like Father T. G. Morrow contend that courtship should be at least eighteen months, ideally two years. This is based on a Kansas City study that Father Morrow suggested.
[36] Ripperger, "Four Stages of Courtship."
[37] Ripperger, "Four Stages of Courtship."

Four Stages of Courtship
According to Father Chad Ripperger

Stages	Definition	Length	Goal
Friendship	A period of getting to know someone with no physical affection; this occurs in a group setting.	3 to 6 months	To determine the other person's virtue
Courtship	Man asks father's permission to court his daughter. A period of exclusivity with no physical affection; this occurs in a group setting.	3 to 6 months	To grow in self-denial
Betrothal/ Engagement	Man asks father's permission to marry his daughter. Small signs of affection, such as holding hands and quick pecks on the cheek and even lips. Couple spends more time together in a group setting.	3 to 6 months	To grow in moderation together
Marriage	The final stage of courtship where physical affection including conjugal rights is permitted.	Lifetime	To become saints together and to get to heaven

There are many important virtues to look for in your spouse, but they do not make up the heart of this book. Virtues top the checklist when sizing up a potential spouse during the courtship process. They become a "sort of examination of your future spouse." Although this book is about the stories of saints and how they met, it would be an oversight not to touch briefly on the virtues that one ought to look for in a spouse. First is the virtue of charity. A man or woman who does not love God cannot love his neighbor, and whoever does not love their neighbor cannot love God (see 1 Jn. 4:20). A man who loves his spouse more than God does not truly love her. He must love God more than her.

Chastity, the perfect integration of body and soul, is nonnegotiable when finding a spouse. Those who are addicted to pornography without fighting this evil can never genuinely love, because their heart is divided. Pornography is one of the greatest threats to marriages today. At the same time, couples' actions need to be pure toward one another.

The virtue of humility means having an accurate picture of oneself and how one stands in relation to God. It is the opposite of pride. A proud spouse will make for a hellish marriage. He or she will rarely admit they are wrong. They resemble Satan who came not to serve but to be served.

Possession of the virtue of patience, an exercise of the cardinal virtue of fortitude, is a strong indicator of whether you and your spouse will have a blessed marriage. Specifically, how well does your future spouse suffer patiently? Marriage is the school of suffering. From potential child loss to job loss, not to mention being purified daily by your spouse's weaknesses and flaws, you will be tested like never before. Find someone who does not flee from the cross but, rather, embraces it.

It is worth mentioning the importance of temperaments in relationships. Temperaments refer to our natural tendencies and reactions to situations. The notion of temperaments existed long before Christ, going as far back as Hippocrates (c. 460–377 BC), who is often credited with helping to define them. Although we are born with temperaments (there are four of them: choleric, melancholic, sanguine, and phlegmatic), they can change over time. Knowing your temperament and your spouse's temperament can lead to a more tranquil marriage, especially when it comes to communication.

In the book *The Temperament God Gave You*, Art and Laraine Bennett remind us that, "Temperament differences are not *in themselves* enough to make or break a relationship."[38] The authors further declare, "Many people marry someone of the opposite temperament, and do manage to build happy, long-lasting marital relationships. That's because what is most important is that your spouse's *values and beliefs*—not his temperament—are the same as yours. Yet complementarity in temperament is generally a boon to relationships, provided the partners develop mutual respect for their different styles. A family is enriched by having varied approaches and perspectives on a situation."[39] Temperaments are not deal breakers, but they should be given greater importance than a person's physical features. At the same time, temperaments should be subordinate to virtue. But in the end, "grace builds

---

[38] Bennett and Bennett, *The Temperament God Gave You*, 79.
[39] Bennett, 80.

upon nature"[40] as Saint Thomas Aquinas said. If a couple is willing to grow in holiness and love, God can work miracles no matter their differences.

Although not exactly mirroring the four stages of courtship, the following stories from Scripture, the saints, and those on their path to saintliness, provide a unique glimpse into how some of the saints (and those who raised saints) met their spouses. Experiencing a sacrificial and holy marriage until death is only possible with God's grace. And these saints reveal firsthand that "with God all things are possible" (Matt. 19:26). For those called to marriage, God expects nothing less than a saintly marriage, which begins by studying some of the greatest courtships and marriages in the history of the Church.

---

[40] Quoted in Bennett, 3.

CHAPTER 2

BIBLICAL COURTSHIP

"Behold my beloved speaketh to me: Arise, make haste, my love,
my dove, my beautiful one, and come."

—Canticle of Canticles 2:10

THE BIBLE IS God's greatest love letter to His people. This is seen wonderfully in the Canticles, or Song of Songs. The above quote, often read at weddings, reflects words from the Divine Lover who is constantly pursuing us. The Word of God loved man so excessively that He became flesh, taking the form of a child and then dying to prove His love. His love letter was not written in mere words, but penned by His very precious blood, the ink of salvation. But He did not stop there. He instituted the Holy Eucharist to remain with us always.

Our Eucharistic Lord is the greatest pursuer of men, the Hound of Heaven, who knocks at the door of our hearts day and night. In the Eucharist, Christ reveals how to pursue a woman, that is, with humility, courage, gentleness, and sacrificial love. If any man wants to know how to pursue a woman, he ought to spend significant time with Christ in the Holy Eucharist and read His Holy Word. Saint Paul sets up the foundation of courtship with these words: "Charity (or love) is patient, is kind: charity envieth not, dealeth not perversely; is not puffed up" (1 Cor. 13:4).

Although the Bible is filled with numerous marriage stories, including the most memorable one in the New Testament at Cana, this chapter will focus on just four courtships, two of which require private revelation to fill in the gaps of known history.

BOAZ AND RUTH

Saint Matthew's Gospel begins with Jesus's genealogy. The forty-two names listed represent a microcosm of the entire human race, sinners and saints alike. Jesus's family tree is filled with good and bad fruit. Two names stand out among this lineage: Boaz and Ruth.[41] Ruth is one of just five women mentioned in Jesus's genealogy. Boaz and Ruth's courtship and marriage is one of the most beautiful of the ancient love stories recorded in Sacred Scripture, for it tells the story of perseverance, redemption, suffering, and patience. Written around the sixth to fourth century BC, this love story predates every famous love story, from Romeo and Juliet to Mr. Darcy and Miss Elizabeth from *Pride and Prejudice.*

God does not promise married couples a long, happy life together; rather, He promises the cross on earth and then heaven for those who remain faithful. But at the same time, He longs for us to live heaven now through a life of virtue, the

---

[41] The Douay-Rheims Bible uses the name Booz, but most translations use Boaz. Since Boaz is the more common spelling, it will be used here. However, the Douay-Rheims passages will retain the spelling Booz.

only life that brings true peace and true joy. As Christ said, "I am come that they may have life, and may have it more abundantly" (John 10:10). God longs for every married couple to have a sacred and joyous marriage. But to appreciate any blessing in life, sometimes God makes us pass through trials. For what saint can deeply appreciate heaven if he has never suffered trials, temptations, and sorrows?

Throughout Sacred Scripture, we hear stories of natural disasters: floods, pestilence, famine. One particular famine set things in motion for two of Jesus's ancestors. Because of a famine in Bethlehem, Elimelech and his wife Naomi[42] and their two sons, Mahalon and Chelio, left their native land, a land that worshipped the one true God, for a foreign land of many gods. The treacherous fifty-mile trek would have taken them around seven to ten days by foot. Unfortunately, Elimelech died soon after arriving in Moab. The widow Naomi remained in Moab with her two sons, perhaps praying that the famine would end so she could return home. Maybe she even prayed that her sons would marry holy wives. In Moab, Mahalon met Ruth and they soon married. And the same for her son Chelio, who married Orpha. Nothing is written as to whether Naomi initially opposed her son's marriages to foreign women with foreign gods. But one thing is for certain: Naomi came to love both of her daughters-in-law. For the next ten years, all of them dwelt together in Moab. God brought good out

---

[42] The Douay-Rheims Bible uses the name Noemi, but most translations use Naomi. Since Naomi is the more common spelling, it will be used here. However, the Douay-Rheims passages will retain the spelling Noemi.

of their suffering. But then tragedy struck again as Naomi lost her two sons.

Once Naomi learned that the famine had ended, she decided to return to Bethlehem. But before doing so, she told her daughters-in-law to return to their mothers and prayed that they would "find rest in the houses of the husbands which you shall take"; then, she kissed them goodbye (Ruth 1:9). But Ruth would not leave her mother-in-law. She even renounced her pagan gods for the one true God as Naomi had requested. Ruth's loyalty is held up as a standard for how to care for family, especially our elders.

The two returned to Bethlehem at the start of the barley harvest. To provide food for her mother, Ruth began to pick the leftover grains as permitted by Mosaic law. The fields where she labored were owned by Boaz, a relative of Naomi's husband. One day, as Boaz walked through his fields, he said to the harvesters:

> The Lord be with you. And they answered him: The Lord bless thee. And Booz said to the young man that was set over the reapers: Whose maid is this? And he answered him: This is the Moabitess who came with Noemi, from the land of Moab. And she desired leave to glean the ears of corn that remain, following the steps of the reapers: and she hath been in the field from morning till now, and hath not gone home for one moment. And Booz said to Ruth: Hear me, daughter, do not go to glean in any other field, and do not depart from this place: but keep with my maids, And follow where they reap. For I have

charged my young men, not to molest thee: and if
thou art thirsty, go to the vessels, and drink of the
waters whereof the servants drink. She fell on her
face and worshipping upon the ground, said to him:
Whence cometh this to me, that I should find grace
before thy eyes, and that thou shouldst vouchsafe
to take notice of me a woman of another country?
(Ruth 2:4–10)

Like any good landowner, Boaz kept tabs on who
worked on his land. After all, he was "a powerful man, and
very rich" (Ruth 2:1). And he knew about Ruth's heroic
virtue, for she had left her own people and her own land
to take care of her mother-in-law. Later, Ruth shared her
meeting with Naomi, who then counseled Ruth to "wash
thyself therefore and anoint thee, and put on thy best gar-
ments" and follow Boaz to his resting place (Ruth 3:3–4).
And Ruth answered her, "Whatsoever thou shalt com-
mand, I will do" (Ruth 3:5). Most mothers-in-law would
find it difficult seeing their daughters-in-law remarry
after the death of their son. But Naomi willed the best for
Ruth. And so, prompted by God, Naomi counseled Ruth
to secretly enter Boaz's bedroom. This would really catch
his eye!

Startled by the mysterious lady lying at the foot of his
bed, Boaz quickly inquired, "Who are thou?" Ruth replied,
"I am Ruth thy handmaid: spread thy coverlet over thy servant, for thou art a near kinsman" (Ruth 3:9). Ruth did
not try to seduce Boaz, for she lived chastely. Instead, Ruth
asked Boaz to protect her and ultimately take her as his
wife. Boaz was honored by Ruth's request, especially since

Ruth did not chase after younger men after her husband passed away. Boaz could have easily dismissed Ruth for innocently inviting herself into his private quarters, but he did not. Rather, Boaz, as the "kinsmen redeemer," freed Ruth and Naomi from their current captivity of poverty, an act which foreshadowed Christ's redemption and mercy.

There is also another twist. Boaz did not have first rights to Ruth because another kinsman was set to inherit Naomi's land and, thus, have Ruth. Boaz could have married Ruth secretly, but instead, he approached the man in all sincerity and informed him he had first rights to purchase the land. This man renounced his right to Naomi's land and Ruth. Hence, Boaz's integrity and patience paid off.

Boaz and Ruth married, and God blessed them with a son named Obed, who became the grandfather of King David. After she lost her first husband, Ruth may have wondered if she would ever find true love again, especially since she was destitute and had to provide for her mother-in-law. She seemed to have nothing to offer a man. But Boaz looked deeper. He saw a woman of virtue, not a woman with no dowry and a needy mother-in-law. In essence, Ruth embodied the words of the Proverb: "Favour is deceitful, and beauty is vain: the woman that feareth the Lord, she shall be praised. Give her of the fruit of her hands: and let her works praise her in the gates" (Prov. 31:30–31). A man that fears the Lord should also be praised. In the end, Ruth married an older man, a man of virtue. Perhaps Boaz longed to be married at a younger age, but the famine drove away potential wives as many people fled from Bethlehem. God's plan for marriage did not happen as Boaz and

Ruth initially imagined. He led them on a path unknown to them. Their story shows us that those who trust in God will not be put to shame (see Ps. 25:1).

TOBIAS AND SARAH

One of the least known love stories in the Bible outside of the Catholic Church is the story of Tobias and Sarah found in the Book of Tobit. The Book of Tobit is one of seven books along with the Books of Wisdom, Ecclesiasticus, Judith, Baruch, First and Second Machabees and segments of Esther and Daniel that make up the deuterocanonical books, or books located only in the second or Greek list of canonical Scriptures. The Catholic Church recognized the Greek Septuagint Bible at the Council of Rome in 382, while the Protestants later accepted the shorter Hebrew Canon without the deuterocanonical books.

Because it is such a fascinating love story, the Book of Tobit is one of the most widely used first readings at Catholic weddings. Sadly, few Protestants have heard it. This short Jewish story took place around the eighth century BC. The plot centers on Tobias being sent to Media by his father, Tobit, to retrieve money. While Tobias thought he was going to fetch his father's money, God had something greater in store. This grander plan was manifested right from the start of the journey, as Tobias's guide, Azarias, whom he thought was his kinsman, was later revealed to be the archangel Raphael.

When Tobias arrived in Media, Azarias informed him that it was his right to marry Sarah, his cousin and closest relative. Ironically, all of Sarah's seven previous husbands were killed on their wedding night by the demon Asmodeus. In response to this news, Tobias was justifiably afraid. In his words, "Now I am the only son my father has, and I am afraid that if I go in I will die as those before me did, for a demon is in love with her, and he harms no one except those who approach her. So now I fear that I may die and bring the lives of my father and mother to the grave in sorrow on my account. And they have no other son to bury them" (Tb 6:14, RSV).

Azarias assures Tobias with these angelic words—words of peace and courage:

> Do you not remember the words with which your father commanded you to take a wife from among your own people? Now listen to me, brother, for she will become your wife; and do not worry about the demon, for this very night she will be given to you in marriage. When you enter the bridal chamber, you shall take live ashes of incense and lay upon them some of the heart and liver of the fish so as to make a smoke. Then the demon will smell it and flee away, and will never again return. And when you approach her, rise up, both of you, and cry out to the merciful God, and he will save you and have mercy on you. Do not be afraid, for she was destined for you from eternity. You will save her, and she will go with you, and I suppose that you will have children by her. When Tobi'as heard these things, he fell in love with her and yearned deeply for her. (Tb 6:15–17, RSV)

Outside of the archangel Gabriel's words to Mary, these might be the most beautiful words ever spoken by an archangel to a human person. These words should echo in the hearts of every man pursuing a woman: Saint Raphael foretold Tobias's vocation, thus empowering him to fulfill his divine calling with courage. For those called to marriage, God desires to give every grace necessary to reach heaven. Finding a helpmate is one of the greatest graces.

In the Douay-Rheims translation, Saint Raphael advised Tobias and Sarah to fast and pray for three days before they consummate their love (see Tob. 6:18). This certainly helped drive away the demon! One of the most widely used first readings at Catholic weddings comes from the Book of Tobit chapter eight when Tobias and Sarah beg the Lord to have mercy on them before consummating their love. Tobias prays, "And now, O Lord, I am not taking this sister of mine because of lust, but with sincerity. Grant that I may find mercy and may grow old together with her" (Tb 8:7, RSV).

Ironically, Sarah's father had started to dig a grave for his son-in-law. But God had mercy on Tobias and Sarah as the demon was bound up by Saint Raphael. Tobias and Sarah were not the only ones who praised God. Tobias's father Tobit, who had been temporarily blind and was now healed due to the instruction of Saint Raphael, offered some of the most beautiful words a father can say to his daughter-in-law: "Welcome, daughter! Blessed is God, who has brought you to us, and blessed are your father and your mother" (Tb 11:17, RSV).

The Book of Tobit reveals many striking truths. One unforgettable truth came from the mouth of Saint Raphael:

"Do not be afraid, for she was destined for you from eternity" (Tb 6:17, RSV). Make no mistake, God is the "Divine Matchmaker." It was God who destined Tobias's and Sarah's marriage from all eternity. Sometimes we do not understand when relationships fall apart. Certainly, many of us would like an archangel to introduce us to our spouse, but then again, how many men would marry a woman whose seven previous husbands died on their wedding night? The odds were stacked against Tobias. Sometimes the odds are stacked against many people discerning marriage. Many men are turned down repeatedly and soon give up, while many women are hard-pressed to find a solid Catholic man.

Regardless, we must hold on to the truth that if we are called to marriage, God has someone for us. If you are looking for an incredible, true love story, only fourteen chapters long, start with the Book of Tobit. Never doubt that your guardian angel and Saint Raphael, the patron of finding one's spouse, desire you to find your spouse even more than you do.

At the same time, Saint Raphael, whose name means "God has healed," also seeks to heal every person who is preparing for marriage or is married. Just as Saint Raphael was an instrument of healing of Tobit's blindness, so God wants to use him to help heal our woundedness. Many people marry with past wounds, which, if ignored, will only hurt their spouse. Some couples can bring healing to one another, but the truth is that the more healing we experience before our marriage and the more we invite the Lord and the saints into our wounds, the healthier our future marriages will be.

Finally, the beauty of Sacred Scripture is that it continues to unfold in our lives. While the love story of Tobias and Sarah occurred thousands of years ago, similar stories live throughout the Church's history as will be seen in the lives of the saints.

SAINTS JOACHIM AND ANNE

God cares about every marriage, but even more so when it involves His coming into the world. Every year on July 26, the Church celebrates the feast day of Saints Joachim and Anne. They hold the distinction of being the only couple in the world whose child, Mary, was conceived without original sin. But even more importantly, their grandson is Jesus! One would think that such holy people would be mentioned in Scripture, but this is not the case. Instead, Saint Matthew's genealogy account mentions Jacob, the father of Joseph, and traces his lineage through his father's side (see Matt. 1:16). And yet, Saints Joachim and Anne's hidden role in salvation history is undeniable. What we know about this holy couple comes from the "Protoevangelium of James"—one of the apocryphal writings and what is a form of private revelation. This combined with the mystical visions of Blessed Anne Catherine Emmerich, an Augustinian Religious Sister, offers unique insights into the parents of the Blessed Mother.[43]

---

[43] Our Lord revealed His entire life to Blessed Anne Catherine Emmerich, which can be found in TAN Books' four-volume set, *The Life of Jesus Christ and Biblical Revelations*. These works have received approval from many bishops and priests.

Saint Anne, a descendant of a line of prophets and holy souls, was raised in the temple from age five to seventeen. On her mother's deathbed, Anne was given charge of her siblings and was commanded to marry, "for she was a vessel of promise."[44]At the age of nineteen, Anne married Joachim.[45] Normally, Anne would have chosen her spouse from the Levites of the tribe of Aaron, as her relatives had done, but God led her to marry Joachim from the house of David. It was said that Anne had many potential candidates for marriage. According to Blessed Anne Catherine Emmerich's vision of Anne, "she was not strikingly beautiful, though prettier than some others. Her beauty was not to be compared with Mary's, but she was extraordinarily pious, childlike, and innocent."[46] A good, virtuous woman is to be praised (see Prov. 31:30). Anne and her daughter Mary were foreshadowed in the beautiful verses of Proverbs describing a holy wife.

Anne could have married almost any suitor, but Emmerich says that she chose Joachim "only upon supernatural direction."[47] As a woman of prayer, Anne was not interested in the transitory realities like physical appearance or wealth, but in the eternal realities of faith, hope, and love. Anne's openness to being pursued by Joachim—described as "poor and a relative of St. Joseph"[48] and a "short, broad,

---

[44] Emmerich, *The Life of Jesus Christ and Biblical Revelations, Volume I*, 125.

[45] Emmerich, 124.

[46] Emmerich, 124.

[47] Emmerich, 124.

[48] Emmerich, 124.

spare man" of virtue[49]—hearkens somewhat back to the story of Samuel and King David. Rather than choose the most esteemed person among Jesse's sons, God told Samuel to anoint David—a young, wiry man (see 1 Kgs. 16:1–12). Anne allowed Joachim to pursue her, for she did not look at the appearance of the man, but according to his heart. Or as the Lord said, "Nor do I judge according to the look of man: for man seeth those things that appear, but the Lord beholdeth the heart" (1 Kgs. 16:7). Virtue always endures.

Blessed Anne Catherine Emmerich also provides some historical background information on courtship and marriage during Anne and Joachim's time. She wrote,

> They were married in a small town that possessed only one obscure school, and only one priest presided at the ceremony. Courtship in those days was carried on very simply. The lovers were very reserved. They consulted each other on the subject and regarded their marriage merely as something inevitable. If the young girl said yes, her parents were satisfied; if no, and could give good reasons for her refusal, they looked upon the affair as ended. First the matter was settled before the parents, and then the promises were made before the priest in the synagogue. The priest prayed in the sanctuary before the rolls of the Law, the parents in their accustomed place, while the young couple in an adjoining apartment deliberated in private over their intention and contract. When they had taken their determination, they declared it

---

[49] Emmerich, 125.

to their parents. The latter again conferred with the priest, who now went to meet the couple outside the sanctuary. The nuptial ceremony was celebrated the next day.[50]

After their marriage, the couple lived with Anne's father for seven years before finding their own place.[51] Their greatest legacy was the fruit of their marriage, Mary, who cooperated with God to produce the greatest fruit, Jesus. Yes, long before Jesus came into the world, God was raising His own virtuous ancestors—one holy courtship and marriage at a time.

SAINTS JOSEPH AND MARY

Of all the courtships and marriages in the Bible or in the history of the world, none is greater than that of Saints Joseph and Mary. It was the union that the prophets longed for, the one the angels rejoiced over. Above all, it was the one that God had plotted before the world began. This one marriage would change the course of human history by welcoming the Savior of the universe. As such, it was a covenant that would transform every marriage from that point forward. Now couples would see that their marriage was not just about themselves or even about their own children; rather, their marriage was about bringing Christ's life into this world. It was about becoming another tiny "holy family" where Christ rests at the center of everything.

---

[50] Emmerich, 125.
[51] Emmerich, 127.

So important was Joseph and Mary's espousal that it has its own liturgical feast day—the Feast of the Holy Spouses, traditionally celebrated on January 23.[52] Though not celebrated universally, this feast stretches back to the fifteenth century.

Even though Joseph and Mary's union was the most important marriage in the history of the world, Sacred Scripture provides no details surrounding their meeting. As a result, we shall turn to private revelation again, to the great mystic Venerable Mary of Agreda[53] to provide additional information. Around the age of thirteen, Our Lady had a vision of God. He told her that she was to be married. But Our Lady, who had promised her virginity to God, pleaded to God that she be allowed to remain a virgin for life.

At the same time, God spoke in a dream to Saint Simeon, the high priest, and "commanded him to arrange for the marriage of Mary, the daughter of Joachim and Anne of Nazareth; since He regarded her with special care and love."[54] God also told Saint Simeon and his fellow priests and scholars to select the worthiest spouse for Mary. This time, Mary pleaded before God's representative to allow her to remain a perpetual virgin,[55] but then resigned her-

---

[52] I am indebted to Father Donald Calloway's book, *Consecration to Saint Joseph: The Wonders of Our Spiritual Father,* for highlighting the importance of Joseph and Mary's espousal.

[53] Venerable Mary of Agreda was a Spanish nun born in 1602. She had many gifts, including that of bilocation consisting of hundreds of visits to Texas Native Americans.

[54] Mary of Agreda, *The Mystical City of God*, 136.

[55] At this time, Mary was not sure how she could be married and still remain a perpetual virgin. God would later enlighten her.

self to Saint Simeon's direction with these words: "But thou my master, who art to me in place of God, wilt teach me what is according to His holy Will."[56] Saint Simeon reminded Mary that marriage is a path of perfection, perhaps even the path to bear the Messiah, with the following words:

> Remember, that no maiden of Israel abstains from marriage as long as we expect the coming of the Messias conformably to the divine prophecies. Therefore all who obtain issue of children among our people esteem themselves happy and blessed. In the matrimonial state thou canst serve God truly and in great perfection; and in order that thou mayest obtain a companion according to the heart of God and who will be comfortable to thy wishes, we will pray to the Lord, as I have told thee, asking Him to single out a husband for thee, who shall be pleasing to Him and of the line of David; do thou also pray continually for the same favor, in order that the Most High may favor thee and may direct us all.[57]

During this time of uncertainty, Mary intensified her prayers, begging God that she might fulfill His will. Our Lord appeared to Mary and told her that He would enlighten the priests and that He would "find for thee a perfect man conformable to my heart and I will choose him from the number of my servants."[58]

---

[56] Mary of Agreda, *The Mystical City of God*, 136.
[57] Mary of Agreda, 136.
[58] Mary of Agreda, 136.

While praying in the temple, God made known to the priests that Joseph was to be Mary's spouse through the following process. The priests gave each unmarried man a stick and urged them all to pray in unison to make known Mary's spouse. Only Joseph's staff "was seen to blossom" and a dove rested on his head.[59] Joseph also heard an interior voice from God saying to take Mary as his spouse. According to Mary of Agreda, Joseph was thirty-three years old and "of handsome person and pleasing countenance, but also of incomparable modesty and gravity; above all he was most chaste in thought and conduct, and most saintly in all his inclinations. From his twelfth year he had made and kept a vow of chastity."[60] Likewise, Mary was "more pure than the stars of the firmament."[61] The priests solemnly declared that God had chosen Saint Joseph as Mary's spouse. Mary espoused Joseph around the age of fourteen.

Following their espousal, Joseph and Mary returned to Nazareth where they both shared their desires to fulfill their private vows of perpetual chastity.[62] Joseph continued his work as a carpenter and together the couple lived

---

[59] Mary of Agreda, 138.

[60] Mary of Agreda, 137.

[61] Mary of Agreda, 138.

[62] In this context, chastity is referring to virginity, though the two are different, but related. Chastity is a virtue that moderates the sexual senses and is a form of temperance. A chaste person may or may not be a virgin. The Church states that Mary was a perpetual virgin, and most saints, including Jerome, argue the same for Saint Joseph. The belief that Saint Joseph was a widower before his marriage to Mary comes from apocryphal works.

a simple and poor lifestyle because "the Lord did not wish them to be rich, but poor and lovers of the poor."[63] And thus they became the most compatible match and the greatest marriage in the history of the world. Saint Joseph was the only one of Mary's potential suitors who "thought himself unworthy" of her.[64]

Humility, obedience, and conforming to God's will through ardent prayer were the cornerstones of Joseph and Mary's marriage. Mary of Agreda noted there "arose between the two Spouses a holy contest, who should obey the other as superior. But she, who among the humble was the humblest, won in the contest of humility; for as the man is the head of the family, she would not permit this natural order to be inverted. She desired in all things to obey her spouse, asking him solely for permission to help the poor, which the Saint gladly gave."[65]

When Saint Paul declares, "Therefore as the church is subject to Christ, so also let the wives be to their husbands in all things" (Eph. 5:24), was he not mysteriously writing about Joseph and Mary's holy marriage? And in turn, Joseph was the archetype for Saint Paul's words, "Husbands, love your wives, as Christ also loved the church, and delivered himself up for it" (Eph. 5:25). Before Christ laid down His life for the Church, He witnessed Joseph laying down his life for their domestic Church in Nazareth. Therefore, Saint Paul's somewhat contentious statement

---

[63] Mary of Agreda, *The Mystical City of God*, 142.
[64] Mary of Agreda, 138.
[65] Mary of Agreda, 142.

was not only fulfilled by Christ, but was also lived out by Joseph and Mary.

As Saint Joseph and Mary's marriage progressed, God enlightened Saint Joseph concerning his wife's virtues, leading him to thank God even more, but also increasing in his heart "a holy fear and reverence greater than words could ever suffice to describe."[66] Before Joseph's eyes was the most beautiful and holiest woman who ever lived. A woman more glorious than the Ark of the Covenant or the Ten Commandments, for soon God would choose her womb to become His very temple on Earth. And should not every husband carry the same sentiments in his heart? "Before my eyes is the most beautiful woman in the world, the woman God has chosen for me—the woman whose very womb could become a dwelling for an immortal soul one day." Beauty is not in some far distant land, but right in front of our eyes.

Mary of Agreda also notes that God gave Saint Joseph a special grace upon marriage, so that his natural inclinations were protected. Can you imagine for a second what Joseph saw each time he peered into the eyes of his beloved, Mary? He saw something so pure and holy that were it not for God's grace, he might have died. Because Mary is the mirror of God, Joseph experienced a foretaste of the Beatific Vision. Just as they say the eyes are the window to the soul, so Mary's eyes were the window to the Blessed Trinity. For whoever gazes upon Mary, gazes upon God's most beloved daughter and queen, whose radiance

---

[66] Mary of Agreda, 142.

surpasses every beauty in this life. Yes, whoever sees Mary sees God's splendor shining forth, more so than any other creature. For Mary's entire body and soul "magnify the Lord" (Luke 1:46).

One might wonder if Mary experienced some letdown after God called her to marriage. After all, she had longed to remain in the temple and to be consecrated to God alone since her youth. Marriage was never her desire, but it became her desire when God willed it.

In a stirring message, Our Lady reminded Mary of Agreda that marriage is a clear path to perfection, a path God willed for the two holiest people who ever lived. Specifically, Our Lady declared,

> My daughter, in the example of the matrimonial life wherein the Most High placed me, thou findest a reproof for those souls, who allege their life in the world as an excuse for not following perfection. To God nothing is impossible, and nothing is likewise impossible to those, who with a lively faith, hope in him, and resign themselves entirely to His divine Providence. I lived in the house of my spouse with the same perfection as in the temple; for in changing my state of life I altered neither my sentiments nor the desire and anxiety to love and serve God.[67]

Joseph and Mary entered marriage because God called them, not because it was an afterthought. Even though Joseph and Mary had the holiest marriage, they also

---

[67] Mary of Agreda, 142–143.

experienced many crosses, such as uncertainty, misunderstanding, anxiety, and later, fleeing to Egypt. In fact, Mary's miraculous conception of Jesus led Joseph to consider divorcing Mary quietly.[68] But one thing is for certain, Joseph and Mary trusted in God more than they trusted in themselves, even if God's plan wasn't always clear. And they loved each other madly and chastely because they loved God madly and purely. No couple in the world has ever loved each other like Joseph and Mary did. The more we love God as Joseph and Mary did, the more God allows us to love our spouse as they did: completely, unconditionally, and sacrificially.

Joseph and Mary did not change the world by dying a martyr's death or devoting every waking hour to praying at the temple. They did something far greater: they remained open to God's will, literally welcoming the Messiah into their hearts before welcoming Him into their home. And their relationship set the standard for every courtship and marriage to imitate until the end of time, that is, one filled with charity, chastity, prayer, obedience, and, above

---

[68] Several Doctors of the Church are split on whether Saint Joseph had planned to divorce Mary because he suspected her to be unfaithful. Pope Benedict XVI weighed in on this topic, believing that Mary had not yet conceived by the Holy Spirit. In his book, *Consecration to Saint Joseph: The Wonders of Our Spiritual Father*, Father Donald Calloway MIC highlights the three theories for Saint Joseph distancing himself from Mary and believes alongside with the greatest Mariologist of the twentieth-century, Father Rene Laurentin, that it would be theologically inconsistent for Saint Joseph to divorce Mary given his virtues. It seems likely that Joseph's humility and reverence for the mystery of the Incarnation led him to initially feel unworthy of such a responsibility, which was seen in Mary of Agreda's writings above.

all, surrendering to God's will. Like Joseph and Mary, we rarely see the path ahead of us, whether this person is the one for us, but we must seek God's will above everything. Joseph and Mary did not rely only on their wisdom to discover God's will, rather they trusted in the holy guidance of the temple priests. Hence, one seeking to find a holy spouse would do good to always seek the Holy Family's intercession and the wisdom of holy people in their life.

CHAPTER 3

ROYAL COURTSHIP

"I want to adorn myself, not out of worldly pride, but for the love of God alone—in a fitting manner, however, so as to give my husband no cause to sin, if something about me were to displease him. Only let him love me in the Lord, with a chaste, marital affection, so that we, in the same way, might hope for the reward of eternal life from him who has sanctified the law of marriage."[69]

—Saint Elizabeth of Hungary

OUR WORLD IS enthralled by royalty: kings, queens, princes, princesses. People dedicate their lives to serving them while others spend their lives following them on social media. Movies, novels, and fairy tales have tried to capture the mystique, grandeur, and power of the crown. To be a king and queen is not something one chooses, but rather something one is born into, marries into, or is selected for one by others, as seen in the lives of King Saul and King David.

Long before King David, there was an uncrowned King who existed from all eternity: Jesus Christ, the Second Person of the Blessed Trinity. He alone is the King of Kings

---

[69] Holböck, *Married Saints and Blesseds Through the Centuries*, 198.

46

and the Lord of Lords. With His passion, death, and resurrection, Our Lord ransomed the entire race from sin and death. And for this, His Father crowned Him as the King of the Universe. Long before there was any earthly queen, there was Mary—God's greatest masterpiece. At one time, she was the uncrowned queen in the mind of God from all eternity. By her cooperation with Christ, God crowned His Mother the Queen of the Universe. Now, both Christ the King and Mary the Queen reign forever in "his kingdom that shall not be destroyed" (Dan. 7:14). In ancient history as seen in Sacred Scripture, the queen was the mother of the king rather than his wife since the king often had many wives. The queen mother interceded for her people.

Because of the merits flowing from Christ's passion through Mary's heart, we are "a chosen generation, a kingly priesthood, a holy nation, a purchased people: that you declare his virtues, who hath called you out of darkness into his marvelous light" (1 Ptr. 2:9). We become sharers of divinity, sons and daughters of the King and the Queen of the universe.

In this life, some saints hailed from noble blood, although spiritually every baptized Catholic has royal blood running through their veins, especially after consuming the Holy Eucharist. But unlike many secular kings and queens who ruled as tyrants, these holy souls realized that "unto whomsoever much is given, of him much shall be required" (Luke 12:48). These saints sought to emulate Christ and Mary because they realized who their true King and Queen were. Above all, they realized their crown was a temporary one; their more important one was the "crown of life" prepared for those who "endureth temptation" (Jas. 1:12). Therefore, they realized that their marriage and their crowns pointed their countrymen to heaven, their true celestial homeland.

SAINT ELIZABETH OF HUNGARY AND LOUIS IV

In ancient days, many marriages were arranged for political reasons, especially among Catholic royalty. This custom is still practiced in some cultures today whereby a couple is forced to fall in love out of obedience rather than from matters of the heart. While an arranged marriage can be a recipe for a difficult and unhappy marriage, especially if one spouse had already pledged their heart to another person before their marriage, some saints saw the hand of God behind it all. One of those cases was the princess Saint Elizabeth of Hungary and her husband Louis IV, Landgrave of Thuringia. Though Louis IV is not a saint, he is venerated as one.

Around the age of four, Saint Elizabeth was promised in marriage to the eleven-year-old Louis IV and moved from her native land to Germany shortly thereafter. "She was transported there in a silver cradle lined with silk sheets, together with a sumptuous dowry," according to Ferdinand Holböck.[70] Her foster mother, Countess Sophia, would be her future mother-in-law. In 1221, the fourteen-year-old Elizabeth married the twenty-one-year-old Louis IV. The couple returned to Elizabeth's native country of Hungary

---

[70] Holböck, 193.

for their honeymoon and eventually resided in Wartburg, Germany. Biographer Walter Nigg said it best about this holy couple:

> She [Elizabeth] lived her married life affectionately, with every fiber of her being, and revealed to her husband a sweet womanly charm full of tenderness. Elizabeth's marriage was contracted for dynastic reasons and not on the basis of a personal inclination; nevertheless, the marital union was happy beyond all expectations. . . . Elizabeth was not the sort of wife who is cool and aloof, who draws back like a mimosa at every tender approach or pleads a headache as an excuse; no, she was an extremely warm, affectionate person who hungered for love and intimacy. The spouses had been acquainted since their childhood; the same mother had reared them; and even after their wedding they still called each other brother and sister. From a very early date there was between them a love more intimate than that experienced by many couples who have been married for a long time.[71]

What did their love look like? It was said that this couple "could not stand to be separated from each other either for a long time or by a great distance. Therefore Elizabeth frequently followed her husband along rough roads, on lengthy journeys, and in bad weather, led more by the

---

[71] Walter Nigg, *Die heilige Elisabeth* (Düsseldorf, 1963), pp.161ff, quoted in Holböck, *Married Saints and Blesseds Through the Centuries,* 194–95.

ardor of pure love than by carnal desire. For the chaste presence of her modest husband did not hinder this most pious wife either from watching and praying or from other good works."[72] Clearly, Saint Elizabeth and Louis IV were madly in love. Just as nothing could separate them from the love of Christ (see Rom. 8:35), so also nothing could separate them from one another. The two loves go hand in hand. Those couples who love Christ can never be separated in life or in death.

While Saint Elizabeth and Louis IV loved each other profoundly, they also loved each other as brother and sister in Christ. Their love personifies the words from the Canticle of Canticles, "my sister, my spouse" (Cant. 4:12). When Louis was away on trips, Elizabeth would spend her time in prayer and penance. And when Louis IV returned from his work travels, she "would run to meet him, embrace him with great joy, and with her passionate Hungarian blood, 'kiss him affectionally more than a thousand times on the mouth.'"[73]

Together this couple bore three children, one son and two daughters, one of whom became an abbess. Despite pressure from his inner circle to be unfaithful to his wife, Louis once said, "Let people say what they will, but I say it clearly: Elizabeth is very dear to me, and I have nothing more precious on this earth."[74]

---

[72] Dietrich von Apolda, *Vita S. Elisabeth*, quoted in Holböck, *Married Saints and Blesseds Through the Centuries*, 197–98.
[73] Holböck, *Married Saints and Blesseds Through the Centuries*, 195.
[74] Holböck, 195.

This devout couple reveals another salient lesson: marriage is not a one-time pursuit. When they said, "I do," Saint Elizabeth and Louis IV's love had just begun. Sadly, many couples' loves fade from a forest fire to a flickering candle. What Saint Elizabeth and Louis IV's marriage teaches us is that our marriage vows ought to unfold every day as we seek to sacrifice for one another until death. Like this devout couple, we ought to fall more deeply in love with our spouse each day and most of all with God. Just as we ought to seek the deepest union with God while on earth, so also with our spouse, if God should call us to marriage. This was a challenge for Saint Elizabeth. She prayed frequently in the middle of the night "to withstand an excessive love for my husband."[75] She often felt interiorly conflicted as to whether she loved her husband too much at the expense of her love for God. At the age of nineteen and only six years into their marriage, Elizabeth's world crumbled when her husband Louis IV died from the plague en route to the Crusades. In her tears, Elizabeth said, "Now the world and everything in it that I loved is dead."[76] After Louis's death, she devoted her life to raising her children and tending to the sick and poor in a hospital she founded.

An arranged marriage is the last way most women, especially in an autonomous Western society, want to meet their spouse. Yet, in some tight Catholic circles, there is an unspoken and sometimes even spoken desire among

---

[75] Holböck, 197.
[76] Holböck, 200.

friends for their children to get married. While no money or land is exchanged, something far greater happens, a blessed and fruitful marriage. One of the greatest wishes for any parent is to see their son or daughter marry a godly spouse and share a happy, holy union. Although parents ought never to force their children to marry someone, they must also not be afraid to give their reasons both in favor and against potential suitors, especially if there are serious reservations. Above all, parents must pray for their children to meet a virtuous man or woman, perhaps one who comes from devout parents, even amongst friends. The apple does not fall too far from the tree, and what a blessing for our children to partake of a fruit that comes from a tree known to us.

Like Saint Elizabeth of Hungary and Louis IV's marriage, the Divine Matchmaker can bring a man and woman together no matter their location, age, circumstances, and nationality, especially due to advances in modern technology. What initially began as a political union between Saint Elizabeth and Louis IV became a deeply spiritual and bodily union. God's mode of introducing couples is often very ordinary, such as a homeschool group, school, or parish. Young adult groups or even work can serve as a medium for God to build up His kingdom. God puts people in our path for a reason. Sadly, we are often too preoccupied to notice. Individuals seeking a spouse rarely must scout the ends of the earth to find their mate; instead, before their very eyes could be the one God has prepared for them. And if there is a natural attraction, a desire for virtue and raising children, and above all, a shared pursuit for heavenly things, a couple has the foundations for a happy marriage like so many saintly unions.

BLESSED CHARLES OF AUSTRIA AND SERVANT OF GOD, ZITA OF BOURBON-PARMA

As the last emperor of Austria and the ruler of the famed Austro-Hungarian Empire, Blessed Charles of Habsburg was part of a dynasty that spanned five centuries. This dynasty once helped save Europe from being overtaken by Muslims at the Battle of Lepanto in 1571. To further entrench their place in history, it was Blessed Charles's uncle, Archduke Franz Ferdinand of Austria, whose assassination ushered in World War I. It could be argued that this family saved the best for last, for Blessed Charles of Austria was a man of impeccable character. Together, he and his wife, Servant of God, Zita of Bourbon-Parma (Italy), forged a saintly marriage.

Unlike many royal marriages, theirs was not arranged, although both families knew each other. In fact, the young Charles would often play with Zita's older brothers in Schwarzau (Austria). Zita's father, Robert, the Duke of Parma, and his wife, Princess Maria Antonia of Braganza, had property there. The two would have certainly crossed paths as children. It is beautiful to think that your spouse may not be in some distant land, but directly in front of you, in your town or church, perhaps someone you have known since your youth. But there was a time when Zita considered following a higher calling by entering the convent, as her two sisters had done. Thankfully for Charles, Princess Zita was not called to espouse the Prince of Peace, but a prince of Austria.

Zita described one of her meetings with Charles:

> We were glad to meet again and became close friends. On my side feeling developed gradually over the next two years. He seemed to have made up his mind much more quickly, however, and became even more keen when, in the autumn of 1910, a rumor spread about that I got engaged to a distant Spanish relative, Don Jaime, the Duke of Madrid. . . .
>
> On hearing this, the Archduke came down post-haste from his regiment at Brandeis and sought out his grandmother, the Archduchess Maria Theresa (who was also my great-aunt) and the natural "confidante" in such matters. He asked her whether the rumor was true and when told it was not, replied, "Well, I had better hurry or else she really will get engaged to some one else."[77]

Choosing a spouse is the second most important decision of one's life after choosing to surrender to God. So rather than rushing into marriage, Zita waited until her heart was ready. This is prudent. And clearly, it was not love at first sight. It was a love that grew through the years, especially as her and Charles's families interacted. On the other hand, men tend to move more quickly, as seen in Charles's case.

---

[77] Gordon Brook-Shepherd, *The Last Habsburg* (Weidenfeld & Nicolson Ltd., 1968), 19, quoted in Coulombe, *Blessed Charles of Austria: A Holy Emperor and His Legacy,* 105.

This is how God designed men—to be *initiators*. At the same time, competition often spurs many men like Charles to court a woman with alacrity. It is discouraging and upsetting to lose the pursuit of a woman to another man.

At one point, Charles's great uncle, Franz Joseph, then Emperor of Austria, told Charles "that he must make a choice from one of Europe's other imperial or royal houses. Little did the exasperated old monarch know that his requirements for his heir were to be fulfilled with a love match!"[78] And so the twenty-three-year-old Charles began plotting as to when he would make his move.

The pursuit of Zita ended in May of 1911 when the Archduchess Theresa invited Charles and Zita with her two sisters for a weekend at her lodge in Sankt Jakob im Walde. In this picturesque part of Austria known for its rolling hills, the couple took one step closer to marriage. "It was here, during a week of beautiful May weather away from military duties and official work that Charles was able to get to know Zita. They spent long hours walking together and it was here that he proposed marriage to her. They were away from the nods and smiles and interest shown by others at balls and dances, and could be themselves."[79]

On June 13, 1911, the feast of Saint Anthony, the patron of lost items, Charles found his match made in heaven. The wedding date was set for four months later on October 21. During their betrothal stage, Charles and Zita had

---

[78] Coulombe, *Blessed Charles of Austria*, 105.
[79] Joanna and James Bogle, *A Heart for Europe: The Lives of Emperor Charles and Empress Zita of Austria-Hungary* (Gracewing Publishing, 2000), 29, quoted in Coulombe, *Blessed Charles of Austria,* 105.

two official business matters. Zita was to visit Rome and obtain Pope Saint Pius X's blessing for the upcoming wedding, while Charles would stand in place of his great uncle at the coronation of George V, the newly acceded king of Great Britain and Ireland. Charles had asked Zita to secure the papal blessing for their marriage, which conferred the solemnity of their engagement. There was no turning back.

The pope even offered a private Mass for Zita and her family, followed by a private audience. During this audience, the pope declared, "I am very happy with this marriage and I expect much from it for the future. . . . Charles is a gift from Heaven for what Austria has done for the Church."[80] The pope then prophetically proclaimed that Charles would soon be the emperor, surprising Zita.

As their wedding day hastened, the betrothed couple found themselves occupied with many events. A week before their nuptials, the couple visited Wiener Neustadt for the Austrian Flight Week. While in Wiener Neustadt, the couple engaged in important conversations regarding politics and the Catholic Faith and the rearing of children.

On the eve of their wedding, Charles told Zita something that every man should express to his fiancée: "Now we must help each other get to Heaven."[81] This was the supreme mission of this holy couple, but it was not limited to just themselves. No, this couple would seek to bring everyone they met to heaven, including their eight children.

---

[80] Coulombe, *Blessed Charles of Austria,* 107.
[81] Coulombe, 108.

And thus on October 21, 1911, twenty-four-year-old Charles and eighteen-year-old Zita entered into holy matrimony. Today, it marks the feast day of Blessed Charles and Servant of God, Zita. The wedding took place at the chapel in Castle Schwarzau surrounded by a host of Habsburgs and Bourbons.

Author Charles Coulombe describes that blessed day when two future saints were united in the sacrament of Matrimony:

> Charles was dressed in the uniform of the Seventh dragoons with his Golden Fleece order around his neck, while Zita's satin dress was festooned with Bourbon lilies and she wore a tiara given by Franz Josef. Charles entered the chapel between his mother and the emperor. The celebrant was an old friend of the bride's family, Msgr. Gaetano Bisleti, who was also an envoy from St. Pius X. . . . The ceremony was in French, in deference to the bride's origins, but the sermon was in Italian. Charles had the words engraved in the rings that the couple exchanged: *Sub tuum praesidium confugimus, sancta Dei genitrix* (Under your protection and umbrella, we flee, Holy Mother of God). When the banquet was finished and a fitting toast given by the emperor, the couple departed by car on their honeymoon to Villa Wartholz. The villagers lined the road, and air cadets from Wiener Neustadt dropped flowers on the newlyweds from the sky. The archducal pair made a short pilgrimage to Mariazell to dedicate

their marriage and their lives to the Magna Mater
Austriae. From there, they stopped at the "Gasthau
Elephant" in Brixen in what is now South Tyrol, and
thence to Dalmatia where such resorts as Franz Ferdinand's island of Lokrum beckoned.[82]

On November 21, 1916, Charles became Emperor of
Austria following the death of Emperor Franz Joseph. Just
over a month later, on December 30 at the age of twenty-
nine, he was crowned apostolic King of Hungary. In 1921,
Charles and his pregnant wife were exiled to the island
of Madeira; Charles refused to abdicate his thrones and
so violate his coronation oath. Sadly, he died a year later
of pneumonia at the young age of thirty-four. In his final
hours, Zita held her husband in her arms while saying short
prayers. Besides publicly forgiving his enemies, Charles
said his final words to his bride of ten years: "I'll love you
forever."[83] His last word was the holy name of Jesus. One
thing is clear: Charles was prepared to meet His Maker
through daily Mass and confession. And Charles and Zita
were madly in love with each other. They would live happily ever after, just not in this life. They fulfilled their vocation to get each other to heaven, though Charles's death
came sooner than expected. Love was everything to this
holy couple: love of God, love for each other, love for their
children, and love for their country. In all things, Charles
sought to do the will of God. His motto since his youth

---

[82] Coulombe, 109–10.
[83] "Charles of Austria," Vatican.va, https://vatican.va/news_services
/liturgy/saints/ns_lit_doc_20041003_charles-austria_en.html.

was, "I strive always in all things to understand as clearly as possible and follow the will of God, and this in the most perfect way."[84]

Pope Saint John Paul II beatified Blessed Charles on October 3, 2004. Meanwhile, Zita's cause for canonization has been recently opened. At Charles's beatification, Pope Saint John Paul II declared, "His chief concern was *to follow the Christian vocation to holiness also in his political actions*."[85] Yes, Charles and Zita's zeal for God and His glory permeated everything in their lives. This regal marriage began with a royal courtship, and, most of all, it mirrored the true King of Kings, Christ the King, and His love for the Church.

---

[84] "Blessed Charles of Austria," Catholic News Agency, catholicnewsagency.com/saint/blessed-charles-of-austria-631.

[85] Pope Saint John Paul II, "Beatification of Five Servants of God," Vatican.va, vatican.va/content/john-paul-ii/en/homilies/2004/documents/hf_jp-ii_hom_20041003_beatifications.html.

CHAPTER 4

"Religious Life" after Marriage

"The cross is the bed of my spouses; it's there that
I have them taste the delights of my love."[86]

—Our Lord to Saint Margaret Mary

THE SAINTS DESIRE the greatest intimacy with God, so it only seems natural that they would renounce human love for Divine Love. But sometimes God postponed certain souls' desire for religious life because He wanted them to first experience His love more tangibly through another human person and, consequently, transmit new human life.

Some people might argue that most married saints only became saints because they entered religious life after their spouse died. This proceeds from the mistaken notion that sanctity is only found in the higher calling of consecrated life. But the truth is that the sacrament of marriage helped perfect many saints in the love of God, especially through

---

[86] Thérèse of Lisieux, *St. Thérèse of Lisieux, Her Last Conversations*, 136.

suffering. Yes, God uses everything in the saints' lives and in our lives, both the joys and the sorrows, to bring us closer to Him. Make no mistake, "the cross is the bed of my [Christ's] spouses." The cross is both the quickest and the most difficult path to intimacy with Christ. For, those who embrace their crosses with joy experience the delights of Christ's love, but only a select few wish to drink of Christ's bitter chalice. Our Lord does not discriminate when it comes to suffering.

Just as the Roman soldiers handed Our Lord His cross, so too He selects the perfect cross for us. We can never escape our cross. We may run away from our true vocation, but the cross will find us. Run to the convent because you fear the burdens of marriage and the cross will find you there. Run to marriage because you don't want to give your life completely to God and the cross will find you there as well. In God's mysterious plan, He does not always give the saints the initial desires of their hearts, which for many of them involved becoming a priest or a religious. Instead, He guides them on a different path—the path of marriage. Marriage also has the same end as His chosen spouses: union with God in this life and in the next.

All vocations must pass through Calvary because Our Lord wants us to taste His bittersweet chalice. This allows us to become perfectly conformed to Him in this life, so as to be conformed to Him in the next. With outstretched arms and His head bowed down to kiss His bride, the Church, Our Lord gave everything to His spouse on the cross. His entire being said to us, "I am all yours. I hold nothing back from you. Every drop of My blood is for you alone." And then He looks even more deeply into our souls and says to us, "Will you deprive me of the love you owe to Me?" Our Lord's stupendous love on Calvary continues in the Holy Eucharist, beckoning so many saints to leave all other loves behind for their One True Love, Christ. Our Lord is the greatest spouse. At the same time, God called some saints to experience human spousal love as a preparation for divine spousal love on earth.

SAINT RITA AND PAOLO MANCINI

Since her youth, Saint Rita of Cascia had always longed for the convent, desiring to consecrate her virginity to God. She even spent a year in solitude where she meditated frequently on the Passion of Christ. But her parents, Antonio and Amata Lotti, had different plans for their daughter.

Margherita "Rita" Lotti was born in 1381 in Roccaporena, near Cascia, Italy. Rita's parents prayed for many years to conceive a child and God answered the older couple's prayers with this miracle child. Despite being devout Catholics, Antonio and Amata were not willing to part with Rita when she reached her adult years, especially since they expected her to take care of them in their later years.

When Rita told her parents that she wanted to be Christ's spouse as a religious sister, they were shocked and silent.[87] But then, overcome with tears and sorrow, they pleaded for Rita to change her mind. They also hoped she would ensure the family line continued. Having never disobeyed

[87] Sicardo, *St. Rita of Cascia*, 22.

her parents, Rita could not go against their wishes. And so, Rita agreed to put off her dreams of religious life to take care of her parents. Secretly, she believed that she could still fulfill her desire of belonging entirely to God and serving her parents, even if she never donned a habit. This secret plan brought her great peace and happiness. More than anything, Rita wanted to offer her virginity and heart to God, resolving never to get married.

Rita's happiness was short-lived. Her parents were not content with their daughter tending to them alone. They demanded that she get married and bless them with grandchildren. Her soul was put to the test, "a real combat between her love of God and her love of her parents."[88] Would she once again obey her parents or follow her heart? In reflecting on Saint Rita's parents, biographer Father Joseph Sicardo, OSA, declared, "We would, indeed, be tempted to condemn Antonio Lotti and his wife Amata for arrogating to themselves the right to force the vocation of their daughter, and thus making her the prey of human calculation, did we not believe that God, in His profound and impenetrable wisdom, permitted this, so that His chosen servant Rita, after having been a model for Christian maidens, should also, like Saint Monica, become a model for Christian wives and mothers."[89] God certainly worked through these circumstances. At the same time, parents should never force their childrens' vocations because a vocation is a gift and not a right.[90]

---

[88] Sicardo, 26.
[89] Sicardo, 26–27.
[90] Saints Louis and Zélie Martin, the parents of Saint Thérèse, always

Therefore, children must follow the vocation God is calling them to, not necessarily the one their parents desire for them. Above all, parents should pray for their children to follow God's will.

Perplexed and anguished by her parents' arranged marriage, Rita pleaded for them to reconsider. "My parents, I do not wish any spouse but Jesus Christ. Years ago I dedicated my whole body, heart and soul to His love and holy service. Because you wished it, I gave my promise not to enter a convent. I feel sure, with the help of God, without embracing the marriage state, that I will be able to console and comfort you, and provide for all your necessities, until God calls you to a better and a happier home."[91] Christ Crucified is the only Spouse Saint Rita ever wanted. Sadly, her parents ignored her plea.[92]

It was bad enough that she could not enter the convent, now her parents were forcing her to marry the person they chose for her. Rather than run off to the convent against her parents' wishes (which several saints have done), Saint Rita asked for divine intervention. She retreated to her room where she earnestly begged Christ and Our Lady to make clear the path she should follow, the path that would be most pleasing to God.[93] Rita was overcome with

---

desired their daughters to become religious, but they never pressured them. In fact, Saint Zélie thought all of her five daughters would get married. This was the reason she continued to work from home, to acquire a dowry for her daughters. Even Venerable Fulton Sheen's parents prayed that he would be a priest but never told him.

[91] Sicardo, *St. Rita of Cascia*, 27.
[92] Sicardo, 27.
[93] Sicardo, 28.

perplexity, perhaps resembling that of Saint Joseph and Our Lady, who eagerly sought to understand God's plan. Furthermore,

> Rita knew it would be no sin to marry in obedience to the will of her parents, but since she felt that God had called her, even from her early years, to be His spouse, and since she had responded generously to this summons, by desiring to vow to God the jewel of virginity, Saint Rita now awaited on bended knee the voice and decision of God, which would tell her if she should and could obey the will of her parents without offending the will of her Jesus whom she loved with her whole heart and soul.[94]

Although we do not know whether Saint Rita received a special light from God, she conformed her will to her parents' wishes. Had Saint Rita entered the convent against her parents' wishes, she would have been free of sin. But through intense prayer, Rita realized that "she would please God more by her submission than by following her own will, she resolved, then and there, to obey the voice and Will of God and offer no further opposition to the will and desires of her parents."[95] She willingly and even joyfully sought to enter the married state if it pleased her parents. Only God's grace could turn a heart so set on one path to take another.

---

94 Sicardo, 28.
95 Sicardo, 28.

God offers every woman the beauty of the soul through grace, but not every woman is offered the beauty of outward appearance. Some women are naturally more beautiful than others. Saint Rita was offered both, but she focused more on making her soul attractive for God than her outward beauty. "Beautiful as an angel, modest as innocence and loveable as virtue, Rita Lotti could have had, if she wished, many suitors for her hand. All who saw her could not help being attracted by her physical beauty, and all who knew her were charmed by her native modesty, both in conduct and speech."[96] Clearly, Saint Rita sought to imitate Mary—the most beautiful woman who ever lived in both the order of grace and physical appearance. Beauty of appearance is both a blessing and at times a cross—a blessing because it draws others, especially men in Rita's case, but a cross if not used properly. Too much emphasis on one's outward appearance often leads to the sin of vanity. But Saint Rita only wanted to glorify God with her body (see 1 Cor. 6:20).

Of all the suitors in the town of Roccaporrena, Italy (some ninety miles northeast of Rome), Saint Rita's parents could have chosen any man to marry their beautiful daughter. One would think this devout couple would have sought someone with the same mind and heart as their daughter, someone on fire with God's love, someone who would cherish their only daughter and lead her to heaven. Saint Rita's parents decided on Paolo Mancini, who came from very "influential parents." Paolo was described as

---

[96] Sicardo, 30.

"gifted with excellent parts, but proud and haughty, surly in speech, and by no means a religious man."[97] Unfortunately, Rita's parents were not thinking with the mind of God, but rather seeking to ensure their only daughter's material well-being. One could not fault Rita's parents for finding a man to provide for their daughter, especially for the years after they passed away. However, they overlooked the greatest reality—their daughter was destined to live forever in heaven, not on earth. Saint Rita's parents did not consult with their daughter, for Rita was concerned with a different kind of treasure: the promise of heaven.

While there is no evidence that Rita asked her parents to find a different suitor, one with a deeper faith for example, Rita would have certainly preferred to marry a godly man with no money rather than a godless one with money. Above all, Rita's only concern was pleasing Christ Crucified, who remained "obedient until death" (Phil. 2:8), so she too remained obedient to her parents in all things. By marrying Paolo, Rita had to grow quickly in virtue because their hearts were directed toward different loves.

Paolo's heart remained fixed on the things below while Rita's on the things above. Furthermore, her husband lacked both humility and faith, two essential ingredients for a blessed marriage. So much suffering could have been avoided if Rita had married a more devout husband from the beginning. But this was not God's plan. As seen repeatedly, God's ways are not our ways. Marriage is the cross and the cross is marriage. God drew Rita and Paolo to the

---

[97] Sicardo, 31.

cross, for marriage is a great mystery, as Saint Paul said, between "Christ and in the Church" (Eph. 5:32). Just as Christ's love was consummated on the cross, so too was Rita and Paolo's marriage perfected and united through suffering: the suffering of different temperaments and weaknesses in character, the suffering of different ideals, the suffering of misunderstandings.

Marrying the prettiest girl in Roccaporrena had a negative effect on Paolo. Instead of leading him to a humble gratitude and the exercising of more virtue, it inflated his ego. According to Father Sicardo,

> There is no doubt but that Paolo, who was the very opposite in character and disposition to the modest and gentle Rita, felt highly honored when he learned from her parents that he was the only one, among all the young men of Rocca Porrena, who might pay court to their daughter with the view of leading her to the altar as his bride. Paolo proved himself an ardent wooer, and after a short courtship, he and Rita pledged their marriage vows before the altar of God, in the presence of Jesus Christ in the Blessed Sacrament. The marriage of Paolo and Rita recalls to our minds the marriage of St. Monica, the mother of the illustrious St. Augustine. She was married under circumstances similar to those of St. Rita, and like St. Rita, has bequeathed to posterity a sacred name and memory, both written with letters of gold in the annals of the Catholic Church.[98]

---

[98] Sicardo, 31.

The couple started their marriage on the right track by professing their love before Christ, the Eucharistic Bridegroom, and asking Him to bless their marriage in His holy house. Rita and Paolo would need these sacramental graces to carry them through the trials that awaited them.

Following their vows, they went on a honeymoon, most likely near their hometown. Outwardly Rita seemed happy, but inwardly she was ripped to pieces, "shedding tears at the very thought of losing that pearl of earthly happiness (her virginity), which she had thought to give and consecrate solely to God."[99] The cross came sooner rather than later when Paolo showed his true colors, using "harsh and cruel" words and becoming a "relentless persecutor" rather than a helpmate to Rita.[100] Rather than marrying a thoughtful and loving man, which Rita hoped for, she was now blindsided by Paolo's vicious nature.[101] Clearly, Paolo had fooled Rita and her parents during their courtship. Once married, he squandered their money on gambling and verbally abused her, perhaps even physically.[102] Most marriages would have ended here, but not with Saint Rita. She relied on God to give her the grace of "patience and humility," often remaining silent to her husband's violent outbursts. Rita wanted to fulfill her vows. She sought to please her husband with even greater intensity, thus win-

---

[99] Sicardo, 32.

[100] Sicardo, 33.

[101] Sicardo, 33.

[102] Sicardo, 33. No spouse should remain in a marriage where physical abuse occurs. Verbal or emotional abuse also should not be tolerated, but can often be worked out with counseling.

ning over his heart. It was said that "she remained at home, never leaving it, except to pay a visit to her aged parents or to go to Mass or Vespers. But never did she go anywhere without acquainting her husband, or asking his permission."[103] Always dressed modestly and avoiding gossip, Rita was an exemplar of a faithful wife.

Although this book is focused on courtship, the goal of every courtship is a happy, holy, and healthy marriage—a marriage that ends at natural death, not the courthouse. Saint Rita's virtuous conduct is worth mentioning to other women who might be in a similar situation. With God's help, she transformed her marriage by first transforming her husband's angry heart. And here is how:

> From the very beginning of her married life, her husband Paolo was an obstacle to peace. But Rita met his opposition with the arms of humility and patience which experience had taught her to handle with skill and precision. Whenever her husband became angry, she studied to sweeten his temper; sometimes by silence, and indeed her silence was a wordless prayer that ascended to Heaven; and at other times she waited until his fit of anger was over, and then she would try with sweet and holy words to reason with him and make him understand how great was his offense against God, and how little he thought of his intelligence to allow himself to become the prey and the slave of anger and passion.[104]

---

[103] Sicardo, 36.
[104] Sicardo, 37.

Because of Rita's humility and love, Paolo eventually saw his mistaken ways as he slowly began to "be less choleric and less cruel in his manner of speaking and acting toward her."[105] He repented and sought forgiveness of God and Rita for his cruel ways, and he eventually became the man Rita had prayed to marry. Following Paolo's conversion, God blessed the family with children, which He seemed to be delaying until Paolo was truly ready and grateful for such a gift.[106] The couple was blessed with two boys, whom they named Giovanni and Paulo. From their saintly mother, the boys learned their first word, the holy name of Jesus.[107] The children were raised to be virtuous. Rita was on fire for souls, always trying to help the poor and sick, especially those who had drifted from the Faith.

The family lived a happy and holy life until a terrible, unexpected cross was given to the family. Although a changed man in Christ, Paolo could never escape his past. He had many enemies who could not forgive as Rita had done, and one day Paolo was stabbed to death. Rita never had a chance to say goodbye and her husband never had a chance to receive Last Rites. Upon hearing the devasting news, Rita "was thrown into a paroxysm of grief. She wept as if her heart were breaking, and though her friends and kind neighbors tried as best they could to console her, she would not be consoled."[108] More than anything, Rita wanted her husband to receive Viaticum or the Holy

---

[105] Sicardo, 37–38.
[106] Sicardo, 40.
[107] Sicardo, 42.
[108] Sicardo, 50.

Eucharist one last time. Turning to God in her darkest moment, Saint Rita prayed, "O God, enter not into judgment with Thy servant Paolo, for in Thy sight no one will be justified."[109] Like Christ on the cross, Saint Rita forgave her husband's murderers. Following Paolo's death, Rita became even more zealous for God. But God had another cross for Rita. Having heard her teenage boys discuss seeking revenge on their father's killers, Saint Rita urged them to forgive and not to commit the sin of murder. When it became clear that her sons would not listen, Saint Rita once again went to the only person who could help her. She knelt before her crucifix and begged Christ to "either change the desires of her sons, or no longer spare their lives. God heard the prayer of St. Rita. Both her sons died within a year, well-prepared to go before the judgment seat of Almighty God."[110]

Following the loss of her two sons, Rita's prayers intensified. She sought entrance into a convent of Augustinian sisters, but was refused on three occasions. They told her it was impossible for a widow to be allowed entrance. After imploring God and Saints Augustine, John the Baptist, and Nicholas of Tolentine, Rita was miraculously led into the cloister one night by these three saints. Rita's saintly friends told her that the "*impossible* is overcome in your behalf."[111] The order agreed to allow Rita to stay, and she never looked back. Only thirty years old at the time, Rita would spend the next forty-six years of her life fulfilling

---

[109] Sicardo, 51.

[110] Sicardo, 55.

[111] Sicardo, 67.

her childhood dream of becoming married to the only spouse she ever wanted. Today, Saint Rita is known as a patron of impossible causes (along with Saint Jude) and difficult marriages.

Saint Francis and Eleanora Borgia

Before Saint Francis Borgia became the third general of the Society of Jesus (the "Jesuits"), devoting his entire life to God, he fell in love. But before one falls in love, one witnesses others falling in love. The foundation for one's vocation is often established well before one's birth. In Saint Francis Borgia's case, it was his holy parents, Don Juan Borgia and Doña Maria of Aragón, who prepared their future saintly son for his calling. Saint Francis's father was the Duke of Gandia (Spain), and his mother was the granddaughter of King Ferdinand. Saint Francis's parents were very devout; his mother had a great love for Jesus's Five Wounds, while his father had a great love for the Blessed Sacrament. During his birth on October 28, 1510, five years before that of Saint Teresa of Avila, he and his mother almost died. Prayers were offered to Maria's favorite saint, Francis of Assisi. She promised that if her child was born healthy, she would name him after the seraphic father, Francis. After Francis was born, his mother was intent upon becoming a Poor Clare nun, but his father convinced her otherwise. She wanted to live for God alone.

Pious from his youth, Francis seemed destined for religious life. And yet, his mother thought his devotions were excessive at times. She would say to young Francis:

"A sword and a horse, Master Francis, not pictures and sermons! When I asked God to give me a little son, I wanted a duke, and not a monk. You may be a good Christian and yet a gallant knight."[112] Sadly, at the age of ten, Francis lost his mother, who left behind her husband and four children.

In his teenage years, Francis expressed a great desire for religious life, but his father would not approve. Instead, Juan exposed his son to "every kind of diversion and amusement,"[113] but an encounter with Saint Ignatius of Loyola changed everything. Having been given permission to visit the University of Alcalá, Francis locked eyes with Ignatius for the first time but not the last. Ignatius, nineteen years older than Francis, "took possession of the soul of Francis."[114] The circumstances are worth recounting: Ignatius's own vicar-general arrested and imprisoned him for suspicious charges of Judaizing[115] and influencing two prominent women to forsake their wealth for a difficult pilgrimage.[116] These accusations were ultimately deemed false. Still, Ignatius's "utmost serenity and a greatness of soul beyond reach of persecution and insult" made a profound impression on Francis.[117] Francis knew he wanted to be like Ignatius, possibly even follow him, but he didn't know how or when. Perhaps he considered renouncing his

---

[112] Clarke, *The Life of St. Francis Borgia of the Society of Jesus*, 20.

[113] Clarke, 25.

[114] Clarke, 27.

[115] Judaizers referred to Jewish Christians who held that circumcision and observing the Mosaic Law were necessary for salvation.

[116] Clarke, 26.

[117] Clarke, 26.

own father's inheritance as his namesake Saint Francis of Assisi had.

In the year 1528, the eighteen-year-old Francis set off to Madrid to study and work in the court of Charles V, emperor of the Holy Roman Empire and King of Spain. While there, Saint Francis was exposed to many temptations, including gambling and promiscuity, but with God's grace, he "preserved his original purity."[118] He did this through frequent reception of the sacraments, a nightly Rosary, and spiritual direction, all of which he continued throughout his life. Francis overcame the temptation to gamble by reasoning he would be wasting time, money, piety, and peace of mind.[119]

As the son of a duke, Francis was very dignified. He was tall in stature, handsome, and walked with grace.[120] According to a biographer, "his countenance was remarkable for beauty of feature and charm of expression. He had a fair, delicate complexion, bright colour, high forehead, aquiline nose, and small mouth with coral lips, brown hair with a tendency to curl, and those soft almond-shaped grey eyes, which are peculiar to one type of Spanish beauty. Nor were his manners and conversation less attractive than his person. He was not a great talker, but whatever he said was full of good sense and originality."[121]

Saint Francis of Borgia captivated the gaze of many young women. Furthermore, he was a man of many trades,

---

[118] Clarke, 38.
[119] Clarke, 35.
[120] Clarke, 31.
[121] Clarke, 31–32.

including a skilled horse rider, bullfighter, and a musician. His favorite pastime was going out into the country and training birds, particularly falcons. Despite his many secular interests, Francis never strayed from God; in fact, the opposite was true: his secular interests led him to praise God even more. As he once declared, "I received signal graces from God when out in the open country. Many a time, watching the birds at conflict in the air, I bethought me of the work of the devil in destroying souls: what wide circuits he makes in search of them, how swiftly he swoops down on them, how fiercely he attacks them, how he struggles to obtain the mastery, and how vigilant he is to prevent them from escaping from his talons."[122] God's splendid creation was reminding Francis of the great conflict between good and evil.

In his later years, Saint Francis of Borgia accused himself of spending time chasing a "life of vanity and sin,"[123] but his biographers doubt this really happened. When Francis compared his years as a Jesuit with his adolescence, the latter were likely not as pious, as is to be expected. One should always grow in the spiritual life over time. During his years of preparation for his future vocation, Francis lived an exemplary life and expected his servants to do so as well. Gambling, one of the most common activities in Francis's time, was forbidden in his home. More importantly, "Every evening he assembled his household for night prayers and the recitations of the Rosary, each mem-

---

[122] Clarke, 34.
[123] Clarke, 31.

ber of it being required to hear Mass daily, and to approach the sacraments at stated intervals."[124] Amidst the many sensual temptations in Madrid, Saint Francis frequently went to confession and sought the advice of his spiritual director. As a result, according to his confessor, "he preserved his original purity, until he entered into the state of holy matrimony."[125] He wore a hair shirt when faced with grave temptations and strove to avoid anything that would offend the virtue of modesty via his eyes or words.[126] Here is a man who prepared for his vocation like a young soldier going into battle, for true peace follows conflict. Here is a man who resisted all mortal sin, no matter the cost, for the sake of God and for the sake of his future wife.

Around the age of nineteen, Francis moved one step closer to marriage when he began to seek a female companion to help run his household. Although thoughts of religious life and his powerful encounter with Saint Ignatius may have lingered, Francis seemed content with his life, save that of wanting a helpmate. Even Francis's spiritual director seemed to be guiding him to the married vocation. Just one thing remained: Whom would he marry? During his short time in the king's court, Francis had not found a comparable partner, especially one who loved God as much as he did. And, so, Francis let the Empress Isabella, the spouse of Emperor Charles V, know

---

[124] Clarke, 35–36.

[125] Ribadeneira, *Vida del Padre Francisco de Borja*. Madrid, 1594, lib i.c ii. Quoted in Clarke, *The Life of St. Francis Borgia of the Society of Jesus*, 38.

[126] Clarke, 37.

of his desire for marriage. She was only six years older than Francis and a newlywed, perhaps she could assist Francis. After all, she was the most powerful woman in all of Spain and was experiencing the joys of young married life.

Only a few years earlier, the Empress Isabella had wed her first cousin, Emperor Charles V. Upon meeting each other for the first time, the couple was so madly in love that they wed that evening. The Empress brought four noble maids from her native Portugal to assist her in Spain.[127] One in particular stood out, Eleanora de Castro. She hailed "from the most ancient and illustrious families of Portugal, but her beauty of person, grace of manner, and cultivation of mind were on a par with her exalted lineage."[128] Filled with modesty, humility, and piety, Eleanora devoted an hour each day to mental prayer where she contemplated Christ Crucified. She also prayed daily the Rosary and the Office of the Blessed Virgin.[129] It seemed as if the Empress had Eleanora—her favorite maid—in the back of her mind when Francis opened his heart for assistance. His biographer, Clarke, details the event:

> Is it wonderful that when Don Francis confided his intention to marry without delay in the ear of the Empress, her thoughts should turn to Eleanora, and that she should rejoice at the prospect of promoting the happiness of two persons whose interests lay so very near her affectionate heart? We are warranted

---

[127] Clarke, 38.
[128] Clarke, 38.
[129] Clarke, 39.

in going even further than this, for the biographers tell us that the idea of this alliance had ever and anon flitted through her brain, as she watched the handsome couple threading side by side the mazes of some stately dance, and reflected that they seemed, to borrow a homely phrase, "made for one another."[130]

It appears as if Francis and Eleanora became acquainted at a royal dance. As a skilled bullfighter, Francis would likely have had tremendous coordination for dancing, on top of his good looks, charm, and great love for Christ. He would have made a strong first impression on Eleanora. And the same for Eleanora. Her beauty of body and soul quickly endeared Francis to her. At last, Francis could echo the words of Adam upon seeing Eve, "This is now bone of my bones, and flesh of my flesh" (Gen. 2:23).

Although we do not know the extent of the Empress's and Emperor's role in setting up Francis and Eleanora, one thing is worth noting. The Empress Isabella was very prudent in her role as "matchmaker." Clarke further added about the Empress: "She was too wise, however, to give premature utterance to those secret musings of hers. Remembering the proverb of her adopted country that states: 'Speech is silver, but silence is golden,' and knowing that many plans and projects come to utter shipwreck merely because they had been prematurely discussed, she held her tongue and waited."[131] The Empress then conspired

---

[130] Clarke, 39.
[131] Clarke, 39.

with the Emperor, who wrote a personal letter to Francis's father, giving his full support for Francis and Eleanora's courtship. Unfortunately, Francis's father did not approve because "all the traditions of his house warranted him in looking higher for a wife for his heir."[132] Also, he wanted Francis to marry into the Spanish family of Aragon as many of his relatives had done; Eleanora was Portuguese. But the Emperor refused to be turned down, so he wrote again, probably at the Empress's pleading. This time the Emperor and Empress vowed that if the Duke gave his support for their son's future marriage, they would watch over Francis and Eleanora as their own, plus give Francis a prestigious appointment as the Chief Equerry to the Empress or senior attendant. Francis's father acquiesced. Needless to say, Francis and Eleanora would be well-off even without Eleanora's large dowry.

Francis and Eleanora married in Madrid with the Emperor and Empress and many other noble figures present. Though not mentioned, the couple likely wed in one of Madrid's magnificent Catholic churches with all the bells and whistles of a Solemn High Mass. There is truly something special about attending a wedding where the bride and groom love God more than each other, especially a wedding where the couple have saved themselves for one another. As alluded to earlier, Francis Borgia's confessor vouched that Francis kept "his original purity, until he entered into the state of holy matrimony,"[133]

---

[132] Clarke, 40.
[133] Clarke, 38.

referring to Francis's virginity. All of heaven rejoices in marriage, but in an even more special way when two virgins come together.

Outside of the Holy Eucharist, Eleanora was the most beautiful sight Francis's eyes had ever seen. Her love and beauty pointed him back to the source of all goodness: God Himself. After all, marriage is not only a mystery of Christ's love for the Church (see Eph. 5:25) but also an icon of the Blessed Trinity, where husband, wife, and children learn to pour themselves out for each other in imitation of God, who is an eternal exchange of love.

Francis could also echo the words of Saint John the Evangelist, "And I John saw the holy city, the new Jerusalem, coming down out of heaven from God, prepared as a bride adorned for her husband" (Apoc. 21:2). Eleanora was the bride, a mini-Church, chosen by God for Francis, and Francis for Eleanora. Together, they would be God's instruments to lead each other, their children, and all whom they met back to Him. Several saints have described humility as a ladder whereby we climb to heaven. In the same way, marriage was the ladder by which Francis and Eleanora became holy as they climbed rung by rung together.

With so much wealth and prestige from the onset of their marriage, many couples like Francis and Eleanora might soon have become selfish and risked losing their souls, perhaps they might even not have had children or would have delayed children for many years for the purpose of storing up treasures for themselves. In fact, the opposite was the case. The couple used their wealth to help the poor, including widows. They were also generous in bearing eight children. Most of the children were married, and their seventh child, Dorothea, entered the Poor Clares in Gandia.[134]

After witnessing the death of the young Empress Isabella and hearing her stirring funeral homily preached by Saint John of Avila on the vanity of this life, Francis promised God that he would enter religious life should his wife pass away and circumstances allow.[135] Like many people who have met a saint before, Francis felt as if Saint John of Avila "had read his most secret thoughts."[136] While Francis was very devout and would one day become a saint himself, a true saint is never satisfied with his spiritual life, nor does he believe himself to be a saint; he is always seeking to love God more and to love this world less, and always thinks others are holier than himself.

Francis reveals another important lesson: the married vocation calls for daily conversion as much as consecrated life. The latter is often easier because in a monastery or convent one comes face to face daily with one's sinfulness in silence and solitude, while in the married state one can readily escape from oneself in noise and entertainment, and sadly, even focus on his spouse's shortcomings. Francis realized that he must put even more effort into his spiritual life, so that he could become the husband that God had called him to be, which was nothing less than a saint.

Some saints had major conversions from a sinful life, while others like Francis moved from a virtuous life to

---

[134] Clarke, 41.
[135] Clarke, 62.
[136] Clarke, 62.

heroic virtue. According to Saint Bernard of Clairvaux, "There are more people converted from mortal sin to grace, than there are religious converted from good to better."[137] This is an important teaching for those who are married. Although Francis never fell into mortal sin, he knew how great the struggle was to renounce venial sin.

As a married man, Francis spent hours in prayer, often compromising his sleep.[138] He also began to receive communion once a week, more frequently than most Catholics did at the time. His contempt for the world inspired his wife, and, after they became the Duke and Duchess of Gandia upon his father's death, Eleanora renounced the current fashion of extravagant attire, shocking many residents of that city. As she declared, "I should be ashamed to deck myself out in splendid attire, while he whom God has appointed to be my guide and example, goes about clothed in a hair-shirt, and is a model of contempt for the world and of Christian humility."[139]

The couple's marriage was rooted in love and obedience. Eleanora heeded Saint Paul's words for a wife to be subject to her husband (see Eph. 5:22), for "she obeyed him and looked up to him in all things, always considering his will to be, as far as she herself was concerned, an expression of the will of God."[140] And Francis loved Eleanora as Christ loved

---

[137] Dubay, *Deep Conversion, Deep Prayer*, 12.

[138] It is always best to consult with a spiritual director when undertaking penances that could impact one's health. Also, every person is called to imitate Christ, not necessarily a certain saint.

[139] Clarke, *The Life of St. Francis Borgia of the Society of Jesus*, 99–100.

[140] Clarke, 99.

the Church. At one point, Eleanora came down with a bad fever. As her condition worsened, Francis's grief escalated, but so did his intercession. "His prayers were fervent and unceasing; he redoubled his alms and penances, causing many Masses to be said and petitions offered up, not only in the public churches, but in the convent chapels, for the restoration of the sufferer." Francis did not want to lose his spouse, nor did he want his children to lose their mother. Yes, Francis wanted Eleanora to stay with them, even though he certainly remembered his promise to God about entering religious life should she pass away. Perhaps Francis even asked God that He take him rather than his wife.

Before his crucifix, Francis begged God to spare his wife's life and bring her back to health.[141] Francis then heard a voice from the crucifix like that of Saint Francis of Assisi. The voice said to Francis Borgia, "If you wish Me to leave your wife longer in this world, I will do so. However, I warn you that it will not be for your profit."[142] That mysterious voice was none other than Christ Crucified. Instead of pleading further for his wife's life, Francis asked that God's will be done, even if it meant giving up his wife, his children, or even his own life. Francis told the Lord, "From Thy hand I have received it all, to Thee do I give it all back, earnestly entreating Thee to dispose of all according to Thy good pleasure."[143] Such is the surrender of a saint!

A few days later, Eleanora passed away after making a general confession of her entire life and receiving the Last

---

[141] Clarke, 100.
[142] Clarke, 101.
[143] Clarke, 101–2.

Rites. In her final moments, she reflected on the Passion of Christ, her favorite meditation. She even asked for a crucifix to be placed on her lips as she declared, "When I can no longer kiss the sign of our redemption, then indeed I shall be no more."[144] After losing his bride of seventeen years, Francis made a retreat at a monastery where he passed the entire night in prayer and fasting, "prostrate on the marble pavement of the chapel."[145] His prayers were directed not only for his wife's soul, but also imploring God for direction. Shortly thereafter, he entrusted his children to the care of his late wife's sister and set out to become a religious, but one thing remained: acceptance to an order.

Torn between the Jesuits and Franciscans, Francis Borgia was eventually accepted into the Jesuit Order by Saint Ignatius of Loyola. Ignatius told Francis that he must make sure his children were well taken care of before he could enter, including finding a "suitable wife" for his oldest son and suitable partners for his daughters. His other boys would need an income to allow them to attend the university. Francis, a famous Duke, partly chose the Jesuits because he wanted to be "obscure and unknown, and safe from all danger of being elevated to any ecclesiastical dignity, which he dreaded above all things."[146] In 1549, after his children were settled, the thirty-nine-year-old Francis Borgia fled the world and fulfilled the promise he had made to God concerning his religious vocation. Sixteen

---

[144] Clarke, 102.
[145] Clarke, 103.
[146] Clarke, 117.

years later, in 1565, he was chosen to be the third General of the Order.

In Francis's final moments on earth, his brother, who was a priest, asked Francis to impart his final blessing to his brothers, children, and grandchildren. Because Francis's memory was failing, he asked his brother to repeat each of their names, upon which Francis "raised his eyes to heaven, and as each name was mentioned, he asked of God, for every individual, some special virtue or favour, according to the state of life of the person in question."[147] He even went so far as to dictate notes for any relative he deemed in danger. A father never forgets his spiritual and biological children. On September 30, 1572, Saint Francis Borgia passed away at the age of sixty-one. The two women he loved most, Our Lady and his late wife, Eleanora, likely came for him. In that same month that Saint Francis Borgia died, possibly even on the day of his death, there were five or six new stars in the sky called Cassiopeia's Chair, which galvanized onlookers. Many saw this as a sign of Saint Francis's entrance into heaven.[148]

While history will remember this great Jesuit, it is important never to forget that he was once a man in love, who married the love of his life, who in turn led him to the greatest love, Christ Himself. Some of the most beautiful words ever written come from the pen of Francis Borgia: "God has left us from Paradise three things: the stars, the flowers and the eyes of a child."[149] These three things in

---

[147] Clarke, 426.

[148] Clarke, 15.

[149] Gihr, *The Holy Sacrifice of the Mass*, 255.

nature have been untainted by original sin. And Francis knew all of them, especially peering into the eyes of his own eight children. Although marriage has been tainted by sin, perhaps Francis could add that a pure, sacrificial, and devout Catholic marriage can become a little paradise on earth when it mirrors heaven.

Blessed Jacopone and Vanna de Benedetti

Five years after Saint Thomas Aquinas was born, Jacopo, known as Jacopone da Todi, came into this world in 1230. Although not officially a "blessed," the Franciscan Order reveres him as such. But before Jacopone became a Franciscan friar, he fell for the beautiful and pious Vanna, and it was she who helped save his soul.

Born to a noble family like Saint Thomas Aquinas, Jacopone had an illustrious career as a successful lawyer. He was known for being very secular and filled with greed. Vanna, on the other hand, was known for her piety and generosity. She was also believed to be of noble blood. Perhaps Vanna liked the thought of marrying a man of prestige. Or perhaps she prayed that God might convert her husband through her prayers and sacrifices. Regardless, the couple was not a spiritual match. Unfortunately, we do not know how this couple met. But one thing is for sure, Jacopone was a persuasive man; after all, he was a lawyer. He knew how to get what he wanted.

Soon after getting married, Jacopone pressed Vanna to attend a great public feast with him. While there, the stands collapsed, killing the young bride. To Jacopone's shock, Vanna had been wearing a hairshirt as a penance to convert her wayward husband. For the rest of his life, Jacopone likely blamed himself for his wife's death. But he would not let her premature death be in vain, for it led to his conversion. Hence Vanna's life became a sacrificial offering. Perhaps while exchanging her vows with Jacopone, she may have even offered her life if it meant converting her husband. This we will never know.

For the next ten years, Jacopone gave away everything and became a secular Franciscan. Certainly, he had heard of Saint Francis of Assisi, even from those who had known him. Francis died in 1226, just four years before Jacopone was born. Jacopone strove to imitate Francis as he dressed in "penitential rags." Those who knew him derided him and called him "Crazy Jim," which he embraced.[150]

Ten years later, Jacopone was accepted into the Order of Friars Minor. He had been trying for years but his reputation had preceded him. After composing a poem on the vanity of this world and through much prayer (including likely his late wife's intercession), he was accepted into the Franciscan order in 1278 at the age of forty-eight. God had blessed Jacopone with the gift of writing, especially poetry. It is also possible that Jacopone's poetry helped him court Vanna. What woman doesn't love a man who can express his love in this way?

---

[150] "Saint of the Day for December 22," Franciscan Media, franciscan media.org/saint-of-the-day/blessed-jacopone-da-todi.

Jacopone's life was one of two extremes: he went from being entirely worldly to completely religious. While a Franciscan brother (he refused to be a priest, like Saint Francis of Assisi), he was part of a spiritual movement that desired to return their order to its founder's extreme poverty. This had the full support of Pope Saint Celestine V. But after the pope retired, Boniface VII opposed the reformation of the Franciscans. The leaders of the movement, including Jacopone, were publicly critical of the pope, and following a battle between the two sides, he excommunicated and imprisoned Brother Jacopone for five years. During this time of Jacopone's excommunication and imprisonment, which would be lifted after Boniface VII died, Jacopone continued to write, embracing his imprisonment as a penance for his sins.

In his final years, he wrote the famous Latin hymn, "Stabat Mater."[151] As he wrote these words, which we sing so beautifully during the Stations of the Cross each year, perhaps Jacopone put himself in Mary's heart, for both Mary and Jacopone knew what it was like to lose the one they loved. Jacopone was known to weep frequently like Saint Francis of Assisi "because Love is not loved." Jacopone's life reveals a great truth: God is the one who is always courting us, and He sometimes uses tragedy to draw us deeper to Himself, to become His true bride. Although most couples never dream of losing their spouse, especially at a young age, God's ways are not our ways.

---

[151] The "Stabat Mater" is attributed to Jacopone da Todi or perhaps Pope Innocent III.

On Christmas Eve in 1306, at the Poor Clare convent, Jacopone breathed his last breath after he received Last Rites. In the moments preceding his death, he sang one of his favorite poems: "Jesus, In Thee is all our trust, high hope of every heart."[152] He died during the midnight Mass when the Gloria was being sung, some say of an excessive love for the Infant God. How beautiful a thought to think that the Infant God and His mother, and perhaps even his late wife Vanna, would escort this holy man to heaven.[153]

---

[152] "Blessed Jacopone of Todi," Roman Catholic Saints, roman-catholic -saints.com/blessed-jacopone-of-todi.html.
[153] Several attempts by his order have been made to open his cause for canonization. Because Jacopone once opposed the pope, his cause for canonization has been stalled.

CHAPTER 5

The Third Ring
of Marriage

"I think I was born for nothing but suffering."[154]
—Blessed Anna-Maria Taigi

HOLY PEOPLE DO not always have harmonious marriages. When Our Lord told His followers to take up their cross daily, perhaps that includes bearing with one's spouse for those who live in difficult marriages. When a couple gives their consent to each other during the marriage ceremony in the presence of a priest or deacon—often referred to as the marriage vows—they do not know what the future has in store. Thus, this consent is an act of faith and hope: "I take you (name) to be my wife/husband. I promise to be faithful to you in good times and in bad, in sickness and in health, to love you and honor you all the days of my life."

At this most sacred moment, the new bride now has two rings on her finger. The first ring she received months or even a year before. This is commonly referred to as the engagement ring, which is blessed during the betrothal

---

[154] Bessières, *Wife, Mother and Mystic (Blessed Anna-Maria Taigi)*, 36.

ceremony. Now, the groom places the wedding ring on his bride's third finger on the left. Some believe this finger was chosen because the nerve runs directly to the heart. Others, even in the Catholic Church, say the thumb and the two fingers represent the Blessed Trinity, and now, the fourth finger belongs to her husband, symbolizing that the bride belongs to him after God.

What about the third ring? The third ring of marriage will come later, but this ring will be worn by both the husband and wife for as long as they live. This ring is jokingly called suffe*ring*.

Even a holy courtship cannot guarantee a peaceful marriage, but it certainly paves the way for one. A holy courtship is not a "trial run" like those who sadly cohabitate with one another. Some will argue that living together allows a couple to have an escape if things do not go as planned. But where are the commitment and sacrifice? And when you wake up with your spouse on the day after your wedding, what has changed from the previous days other than you now have a ring on your finger? Like any vocation, marriage preparation does not begin when you find your spouse, rather it begins when you find your Heavenly Spouse. It begins with your choices to choose Christ and to follow Him purely and faithfully. And it begins when holy parents help cultivate and till the soil of virtue in the home.

As will be seen in the story of Blessed Anna-Maria and Dominic Taigi, marriage is "for better, or for worse." The spouse you marry will change, just as you will change. Still more, the spouse you marry could betray you. This is the risk, but God is faithful even when we betray Him.

BLESSED ANNA-MARIA
AND DOMINIC TAIGI

Born in Siena, Italy, on May 29, 1769, Blessed Anna-Maria's family eventually moved to Rome when she was six years old. Because of her family's poverty, Anna-Maria was forced to work long hours during the day as a seamstress and by night she washed clothes and made dinner for her family. Though she did not know it, God was preparing her for the crosses of marriage.

Sadly, the family's poverty became a source of great tension, leading her father to often mistreat Anna-Maria. But her parents deserve credit for helping to form her spiritually. After all, this is the most important responsibility of every parent. Though a loving atmosphere was often missing in Anna-Maria's home, they were still a devout family. At the age of ninety, Dominic[155] reflected on his wife's holy upbringing: "Her parents were good Catholics. I am sure they saw to it that their daughter received an excellent education and that she attended the sacraments in due course; I do not know precisely the time . . . but I do know for certain that they used to take her to church very early in the morning to Holy Mass. She went to Confession often—at least I suppose so."[156]

As Anna-Maria matured, strangers began to notice her beauty, leading her to spend more time before the mirror. Vanity became a real struggle for her, but God would

---

[155] The author uses the English version of Dominic while Bessières uses Domenico.

[156] Bessières, *Wife, Mother and Mystic*, 11.

one day give her the grace to overcome this vice. Perhaps she justified this sin as a means to attract a spouse should God be calling her to marriage. Uncertain of her calling, Anna-Maria's confessor "advised marriage since the thought of a religious vocation had not come to her with any real force. Her mother thought the same, but she dreamed of a fairy prince who, won by the charms of Annette, would give them back the lost joys and position of their Siena days. Alas! God sent a porter, an underserving man, the worthy Dominico."[157]

While working for Madame Serra at the Chigi palace, Anna-Maria met her future husband, Dominic, eight years her elder. Unlike Anna-Maria, Dominic came from noble ancestry, but hard times had forced his family to a life well below their class. As a porter, Dominic ran many errands. Like Anna-Maria, Dominic was attractive, with black-curly hair, medium height, and a strong stature. He was a virtuous man but he also had his flaws. According to the Decree of Beatification, "his manners were rough and uncultured and his temperament unamiable."[158] It is further noted of the couple that "he was slow in understanding, pigheaded and turbulent; she was sensitive, pliant and gentle, born in 'the most civilized town of the Peninsular.'"[159] Opposites attract, as they say, or perhaps these differences are ignored when the heart reigns over the head. Father Albert Bessières, SJ, said it best: "As to the differences of temperament, the poor give but a second place to

---

[157] Bessières, 20.
[158] Bessières, 21.
[159] Bessières, 21.

considerations of that kind. All the world knows that no one is perfect and that the cross has to be borne, and then hard work has no time for sentimental theorizings."[160]

Anna-Maria and Dominic's relationship evolved naturally. After Dominic would bring dinner to Madame Serra, he would often converse with Anna-Maria's parents. It helped that Anna-Maria's parents also worked at the palace and the Taigis inhabited the servant's quarters. As stated so beautifully by Father Bessières, "humble folk do not go in for long-winded diplomacy, and Domenico made a shrewd guess that his suit would be acceptable."[161] The best relationships are formed organically, in the school of friendship, the first stage of courtship. A friendship where one need not impress the other person or their parents, but be true to themselves. Genuineness and simplicity are the cloak of the humble soul, whereas flattery and flare are the apparel of a prideful soul.

A French Bishop and Anna-Maria's daughter described Anna-Maria and Dominic's love story with these simple words, "Domenico found favor in the girl's eyes, and the girl in his."[162] Both Anna-Maria and Dominic began to inquire about each other. And their relationship moved quickly. It certainly did not hurt that they worked together. Dominic described his courtship in the following words:

> When I had thoughts of getting married, I made enquiries about the servant of God and her family,

---

[160] Bessières, 23.
[161] Bessières, 21.
[162] Bessières, 22.

and finding that everybody spoke of her in terms of the highest praise, I made up my mind to marry her. She was about eighteen years old and was a maid to one Madame Serra. As I took the dinner every day to this lady, who lived at the Maccarani Palace, I completed the marriage arrangements within a month. After obtaining a promise from the young girl that she would marry me, I asked for her hand of her mother and of her father. I knew that she asked God for light to see His will, and I did the same. I still remember how modestly and tastefully she was dressed.[163]

It is obvious that modesty allures a godly man, while immodesty allures the godless man. Perhaps this is because the virtuous man is drawn to mystery. Furthermore, a modestly dressed woman leaves a man desiring for more, while an immodestly dressed woman unveils herself long before her wedding night. By dressing modestly during their courtship, Anna-Maria protected Dominic's purity and captured his entire being rather than just his eyes. In doing so, Dominic loved Anna Maria entirely and not just parts of her. And in turn, Anna-Maria was able to give herself as a gift.

Years later, some questioned the couple's brief courtship, especially the Promoter of the Faith, also known as the Devil's advocate, who argued against the canonization of a person by uncovering any character flaws or misrepresentations of evidence. From outward appearances, their

---

[163] Bessières, 23.

courtship seemed hasty and rather immature, but not so according to their daughter, Sophie. "My mother told me that if she arranged everything within forty days it was because she did not want to be forever at home 'warming the seat,' but to get on with it once she was assured of a good and honorable future; delay could only bring boredom and danger. She never regretted her action. My father was a rough character, and anyone but my mother would certainly have repented of marrying such a man, but although he tried her patience sorely, she was always glad that she had married him."[164]

A great lesson is revealed through Anna-Maria and Dominic's courtship. There is no "perfect" spouse out there. One must not wait forever to find what doesn't exist. At the same time, one must not settle for an unholy spouse or marry someone with little compatibility, especially if the prospects are slim.

Anna-Maria and Dominic's betrothal took place in November of 1789. Two months later, the couple married on January 7, 1790, in Corso, the day after the Epiphany, by a parish priest of St. Marcel. Despite their poverty, the couple had a splendid wedding reception with food, singing, and dancing.

Prince Chigi gave the newlyweds two rooms that overlooked an alley. Dominic offered one of the rooms to his mother-in-law, while his father-in-law wished to lodge elsewhere. Father Bessières describes how this "damp and dark lodging, made elegant by the cunning fingers of

---

[164] Bessières, 23–24.

Annette (Anna-Maria), in time became gay with six cra-
dles. All the children except the seventh were born there.
Domenico was very proud of his wife, and thought only of
making her an object of admiration."[165]

It is well documented that Anna-Maria eventually gave
herself over to a life of vanity in the first years of her marriage, taking great pains to dress in fancy attire. She did this
solely to please her husband. "All the so-called great faults
of Anna-Maria may be reduced to this: She was given to
vanity and loved pretty clothes."[166] In effect, she loved the
world more than God, which "exposed her to numerous
dangers, but that, as a matter of fact, she did not fall,"[167]
declared one cardinal who knew her. Throughout her life,
Anna's sinfulness and God's mercy were always before her
eyes. She would call herself "a great sinner," even though
she remained faithful to her husband. For the saints, even
their venial sins are a source of constant humility.

Nonetheless, Anna-Maria received the grace to repent
of her three-year frivolous lifestyle. From there, God gave
her many mystical gifts, causing many in the Church to
seek her guidance. Eventually, she became a Third Order
member of the Trinitarians and frequently visited the sick
and poor. She also practiced great mortification, causing
Dominic to call her an idiot for renouncing certain des-
serts that he offered her. Despite Anna-Maria's great love
for the poor and her penitential life, she never lost sight
of her husband and children. According to Dominic, "She

---

[165] Bessières, 25.
[166] Bessières, 25.
[167] Bessières, 17.

kept careful custody of her senses, above all of her eyes. In spite of her vivacity she saw nobody but me, her husband. She never took a walk with anybody but me. I never descried in her the slightest departure from modesty."[168] Yes, Anna-Maria's family was her main priority after God Himself.

Although blessed with forty-eight years of marriage, she suffered greatly in her life from long illnesses, detraction from her foes, and the dark night of the soul for twenty years. In fact, Our Lord once told her, "Your sufferings are essential for some purposes which you recognize, and for others you must be content not to recognize. Your life will be a long martyrdom in support of the Faith and the Church."[169] She died on June 9, 1837— the date that would become her feast day. Pope Benedict XV beatified her on May 30, 1920.

In reflecting on her life, her biographer, Father Bessières, noted:

> The Blessed Taigi alone presents to our eyes the holiness of the mother of many children, of the wife who until death abides subject to a husband, "God-fearing and upright, but unpolished, rough and turbulent." She is a model for all wives, but especially for those who gain their bread in the sweat of their brow; Blessed Anna Taigi was poor. In her the Church will canonize the common life, the ideal of Nazareth.

---

[168] Bessières, 79.
[169] Bessières, 177–78.

Secondly, in this common life Anna Taigi is a victim of expiation; she atones for the sins of the shepherds and the sheep. On the heart of this poor woman the justice of God smites as on an anvil.[170]

BLESSED ELIZABETH AND CRISTOPHER MORA

Born five years after Blessed Anna-Maria Taigi on November 21, 1774, in Rome, Blessed Elizabeth had one of the most difficult marriages recorded in history. But surely, this could have been avoided through a proper courtship? Truth be told, not every virtuous courtship is telling of a strong marriage, nor is every trying courtship a sign of a weak marriage. Sadly, our culture paints a false narrative concerning falling in love. Our culture says your future spouse will only bring you perfect happiness and your life will be a perpetual honeymoon. Or, conversely, that there is no such thing as "true love," so make sure your future spouse has money. Many argue that money will cover a multitude of sins. And, if you fall out of love, then you can walk away through a no-fault divorce.

Before Elizabeth met the young lawyer, Cristopher, she was formed in the classroom of suffering. Although raised by devout parents, her upbringing was riddled with poverty, mostly because of her brothers' poor choices, which also shortened her formation in religion and education by nuns. For several years, Elizabeth grieved over the unnecessary pain that her brothers inflicted upon her family.

---

[170] Bessières, 6.

At the age of twelve, Our Lord commanded that Elizabeth pledge her virginity to Him. Later in life, Elizabeth and her sister, Benedetta, sought admission to the Oblate Ladies of St. Philip Neri. Benedetta was accepted, Elizabeth was not. Much to her dismay, God was not calling Elizabeth to religious life. This led to a period of great sadness and a great resolve to never return to those unhappy years of her home. There was no choice: Elizabeth had to marry. She needed to escape the misery caused by her brothers.

In a biography of Blessed Elizabeth Mora, author Mary Elizabeth Herbert reveals God's perfect timing:

> Her intention (to marry) was scarcely known, when several young men hastened to ask for her hand. At this time she had again partially opened her heart to vanity, and she desired to appear with certain advantages in her new position. But for this purpose it was necessary that her husband should have money; and as none of those who offered themselves were men of fortune, she dismissed them one after the other.
>
> In the end her desire was gratified. The son of Dr. Francois Mora, heir to a considerable property, came to ask her of her parents. Elizabeth danced for joy, and was only happy when she knew that her marriage was definitely arranged. The marriage was solemnized on the 10th January, 1796, she being then twenty-one years of age. Now it seemed to her that she was leaving for ever a state of poverty and trial, to enter into a new world which offered her only pleasure and happiness. Alas! She was far from

suspecting that, on the contrary, she was placing her foot on the way of Calvary, and that the Cross which she then embraced, under such promising auspices, would be in other ways more heavy than that which she was about to leave.[171]

Like Elizabeth and Cristopher, most couples during courtship have a naïve ignorance of the potential sufferings of marriage. Not only does Our Lord call consecrated souls to the cross, but He invites every married couple to enter into this great mystery of love. The only way to find our lives is to lose them, to give them away in sacrificial love (see Matt. 16:25). Elizabeth knew she could never escape the cross, but maybe she hoped for a lighter one. Though nothing is mentioned concerning Cristopher's character, it is clear that Elizabeth overlooked his flaws because of his wealth. Sadly, the allure of future comfort and pleasure beckoned Elizabeth to marriage, not virtue.

Although Elizabeth was misled by money's false promises, her mother was not. Herbert declared, "But if her (Elizabeth's) simplicity and innocence permitted her to be thus deceived by external appearances, maternal instinct had a presentiment of the truth. In the midst of the splendid marriage feast, where everything breathed joy and happiness, her mother, secretly praying, felt her heart struck with a sudden sadness, and seized by a melancholy presentiment, exclaimed: 'Alas! I feel my child will not be happy.'"[172] One of the key aspects of courtship is

---

[171] Herbert, *Life of the Venerable Elizabeth Canori Mora*, 10.
[172] Herbert, 10.

a father and mother's approval of a future suitor. What if Elizabeth's mother had listened to her intuition earlier in the courtship and shared her true thoughts of Cristopher? Perhaps the mother could have saved her daughter from an unhappy marriage. Or maybe Elizabeth's mother did voice her opinion, but Elizabeth did not listen.

In examining Elizabeth's life, Herbert reminds the readers that there is no such thing as a perfect marriage or perfect happiness in this life. "There are certain number of persons in the world on whom everything seems to smile: women whose husbands hold the highest appointments in the state; mothers who may with confidence look forward to the most brilliant future for their children. They are in the full enjoyment of health and beauty, blessed with all the advantages of fortune and position—in a word, nothing seems wanting to their happiness. But experience teaches us that nothing, in reality, can be more deceitful than outward appearances."[173] Courtships can also be deceitful because many couples look only at what they can get instead of what they can give. The only lasting and perfect happiness can be found in heaven, in the Beatific Vision. To believe otherwise is to set your courtship and marriage up for failure.

Partly due to her husband's poor example, Elizabeth was drawn into a life of pleasure and vanity. A brush with death eventually led her to renounce such trifles. Still, Cristopher became very jealous of his beautiful bride and so monitored her activity and her relationships. Elizabeth

---

[173] Herbert, ix.

was even banned from speaking to her own parents. After their first child, this changed, but Cristopher's lustful desires did not, as he cheated on his wife. Tragically, Cristopher deserted his wife and children and wasted the family's money, leaving Elizabeth to raise their two daughters in destitution.

Herbert points out with such stirring words:

> We see, then, that even among the small number of those who appear in a truly enviable position, there are some who are suffering a real martyrdom, which is hidden altogether from the eyes of the world. The shelter of home and the privacy of domestic life frequently conceal the most poignant sorrows. Wives are specifically called upon to suffer in secret. Mothers have peculiar trials, not only in the education of their children, and in their establishment in the world, but from their frequent ingratitude and misconduct after all the care and anxiety which have been lavished upon them from their birth. Sometimes poverty or reverses of fortune come to add their weight to the troubles which so sadly oppress them; and the heaviest burden invariably falls on the wife and mother.[174]

Each couple faces hidden trials. The truth is that marriage is the cross, a real martyrdom. As seen in the life of Blessed Elizabeth, her husband caused her unfathomable pain and sorrow. Yes, those closest to us often cause us the

---

[174] Herbert, x.

most suffering. Not every courtship or marriage will go as planned because of original sin and free will, but God always brings good out of evil. Elizabeth, who also became a Trinitarian Third Order member, never gave up on her husband as she prayed daily for his conversion. God heard her prayers, as Cristopher not only converted, but also became a priest after Elizabeth's death. He would outlive his wife by twenty years.

Couples often fall in love for the wrong reasons, especially when they are not living a virtuous life. But God is faithful, and He can make saints out of sinners and turn back the heart of an unfaithful spouse.

CHAPTER 6

COURTSHIPS THAT PRODUCED SAINTS

"Forgotten people are the mothers of saints, and yet,
by their influence over their offspring, they had an
immense influence over the history of the Church."

—Anonymous

SOME OF THE greatest parents who ever lived were the parents of the saints. On their laps, they helped change not only the history of the Church but also the history of the world, when they taught their children how to pray and how to love God and neighbor. These parents' homes were the first seminary or convent, a school of virtue where they formed saints. Inspired by their parents' godly example, the saints sought to imitate their parents' virtue and share their firsthand lessons with the world.

Even though the saints are remembered today, their parents are (in most cases) forgotten. Most will never have a Church named after them or a feast day honoring them, because they were not canonized. They will pass unnoticed.

But their impact on the Church will be made known one day in heaven.

Just as in apostolic succession, where every bishop can trace his lineage to Saint Peter, so God wants to create "saintly succession" whereby one saintly couple produces saintly children, who then produce saintly children in an almost unbroken line of saints. Saints not only inspire other saints, but in some cases, they give birth to them. When God brings a holy couple together in courtship and marriage, He desires that they love Him above everything and that they raise His children to be saints. And they are able to do this because His grace is not wanting.

Saints Louis and Zélie Martin

Saints do not fall out of the sky. They are born to a family, and, just as they are formed in the womb, they are formed in the domestic Church. When God brings a couple together, He sees the big picture, especially how their marriage will impact the salvation of souls. Our lives are like one piece in God's magnificent puzzle. Make no mistake, God is very much concerned with every life: past, present, and future. The fact that we are on this earth is a miracle, given that many of our grandparents and parents fought in wars that could have taken their lives (not to mention the "war" of abortion that has stolen so many lives).

But another miracle is raising a saint. Saints Louis and Zélie Martin raised not just one saint in Saint Thérèse, but the cause for beatification and canonization for their daughter Léonie was opened in 2015. Stéphane-Joseph Piat, OFM, who knew some of the Martin daughters personally, wrote, "Providence, which was preparing from afar the cradle of Thérèse, guided Zélie Guérin to Louis Martin by subjecting both to the same preliminary experience of aspiring after the complete detachment from the world."[175] Yes, Divine Providence had Saint Thérèse of Lisieux in mind when He was bringing her parents together.

Saints Louis and Zélie Martin both desired to enter religious life, so much so that Zélie was in tears on her wedding night because her dream would never be fulfilled. In time, both resigned themselves to their true calling. It was on the Bridge of St. Leonard in Alençon, France, that the Divine Matchmaker brought two future saints together, who in turn raised one of the Church's most heralded saints in Thérèse of Lisieux (and a possible future saint in her sister Léonie). In my book, *Parents of the Saints*, I describe Louis and Zélie's miraculous first encounter:

> As Zélie Guérin was crossing the bridge of St. Leonard in Alençon, France, on what seemed like an ordinary day, she heard an interior voice say, *"That is he whom I have prepared for you"* as she passed the brawny, noble-faced, and contemplative-mannered Louis Martin. The twenty-six-year-old Zélie's heart began to beat with excitement upon seeing Louis, even though no words were exchanged. After this brief encounter, Zélie longed to see him again.
>
> Although he was a comfortable bachelor at the age of thirty-four, Louis noticed something special

---

[175] Piat, *The Story of a Family*, 21.

about the dark-eyed brunette. Louis confided to his mother that he wanted to formally meet her and not just gaze at her from a distance. There was a mutual attraction, which, according to Pope St. John Paul II, "is of the essence of love and in some sense is indeed love, although love is not merely attraction." Unbeknownst to Louis, his mother had met Zélie a few times before at a lace-making class and was so impressed by Zélie that she had secretly prayed that Louis would someday marry her.[176]

It is worth noting that this encounter took place on a historic bridge, which still stands today. Built in the fifteenth century, the Bridge of St. Leonard is a semi-circular arched structure made of masonry, crossing over the Sarthe River. It would become an apt metaphor as God led Louis and Zélie from a world of singleness and uncertainty to a world of marriage entailing sacrifice, suffering, deep union, and mission. The Martins' marriage would withstand whatever currents flowed through their future vows, namely death, child loss, cancer, an unruly child, and the threats of secularism. Their encounter took place in April 1858, a time when nature was experiencing its own resurrection from winter. It was a time of splendid flowers and a time of falling in love.

After Louis confided to his mother about meeting Zélie, Mrs. Martin appears to have gently pushed Louis to pursue Zélie. Louis was Mrs. Martin's only surviving child. Her four other children had died unexpectedly, so

---

[176] O'Hearn, *Parents of the Saints*, 63.

it seemed only natural that she would want Louis to be surrounded by the love of a family, especially in Louis's older years. No parents want to see their child grow old by themselves. In Louis's case, he thought he had everything: his Catholic Faith, a great career, and recreation (Louis loved to fish), but his mother challenged him not to settle for being single. He was not too late to pursue love. Louis's father, Pierre Martin, had married at the age of forty. Mrs. Martin likely realized that girls like Zélie do not stay single for long. To pursue a virtuous lady requires urgency. I can imagine Mrs. Martin telling her husband to have a little talk with their son.

At the same time, "Louis's mother witnesses to the powerful role parents have in nurturing their child's vocation, especially praying in a special way for their future son-in-law or daughter-in-law that, like their own child, they might be holy and without blemish on their wedding day."[177] Yes, parents have a sacred responsibility to pray not only for their child's vocation but also for their child's future spouse. Although parents should avoid pressuring their children to follow a certain vocation, especially marrying a particular person, they also should not be afraid to embolden them to pursue or be pursued by a virtuous person.

Some believe the interior voice Zélie heard on the bridge was Our Lady's voice with these words, "*That is he whom I have prepared for you.*" Zélie once heard a similar voice after praying a novena to Our Lady after she was turned down from religious life. Specifically, Zélie asked Our Lady for

---

[177] O'Hearn, 49.

guidance as to what to do with her life. In reply, she heard in a distinct voice say, "Lace-making." Our Lord and Our Lady were present in a real but hidden way when Louis and Zélie met for the first time, as they are for every person who seeks the will of God. It was as if Our Lord, who once called Peter and Andrew, said to Louis and Zélie, "Come follow me to marriage, and I will make you parents of a great saint." And Our Lady, like any good mother, was saying to Zélie, "This is the man my Son and I have been saving for you."

Louis wasted no time in pursuing Zélie after their first encounter, thanks in large part to his mother's prayers and advice. Interestingly, Louis and Zélie lived in the same town of Alençon, France, some 107 miles west of Paris. Louis moved there when he was seven years old and Zélie moved there when she was twelve. In this small town (today the population is around fifty-two thousand), it took many years before God arranged Louis and Zélie's fairy-tale-like meeting. They would have frequented the same shops and churches, perhaps unknowingly been in each other's presence. But one thing is for certain: God's timing is everything. Had Louis and Zélie met earlier in life when they were both set on religious life, their hearts may not have been ready for love. Still more, both Louis and Zélie had opportunities to wed others before finding each other, but none proved to be an equal match. For instance, Zélie once turned down a very wealthy suitor, and Louis had the admiration of many women when he lived in Paris. But he remained resolute in his determination to save himself for his wife. Yes, God led this couple through similar but mysterious journeys of suffering and disappointment. And their paths converged at the perfect moment because both Louis and Zélie were not only open to God's will but were waiting patiently for it to unfold.

Shortly after meeting, the couple had an official betrothal ceremony at a local church.[178] They would marry three months after their first encounter in April. Perhaps one reason for their short courtship was that both couples were older. Louis was just shy of his thirty-fifth birthday, while Zélie was twenty-six.[179]

Louis and Zélie Martin were married at midnight (the custom of the day) between July 12 and July 13, 1858, at the Church of Notre Dame in Alençon. Midnight allowed for a more intimate and prayerful ceremony, as Louis and Zélie professed their vows amidst silence and candlelight with their closest relatives and friends.[180] The weekday ceremony was believed to have taken place in the choir behind the main altar with Father M. Frederic Hurel as the presider.[181] It must be noted that the date of their civil

---

[178] "Saints Louis and Zélie Martin, The Parents of Saint Thérèse of Lisieux," www.louisandzeliemartin.org/louis-and-zelies-marriage-meda.

[179] Louis Martin's father, Pierre, was forty years old, and his mother, Marie-Anne-Fanny Boureau, was eighteen years old when they married. Perhaps this was another reason Louis was not in a rush to get married, because his father married late in life. It also seems that both Anne Martin and Zélie Martin looked for a mature man, so hence they married older men. There is no set rule on age difference when it comes to marriage, but the later people marry in life, the more set they are in their ways.

[180] "Saints Louis and Zélie Martin, The Parents of Saint Thérèse of Lisieux," www.louisandzeliemartin.org/louis-and-zelies-marriage-meda.

[181] "Saints Louis and Zélie Martin, The Parents of Saint Thérèse of Lisieux," www.louisandzeliemartin.org/louis-and-zelies-marriage-meda.

marriage occurred on July 12 at 10p.m., which is also their feast day.

At some French weddings at that time, husbands gave wives a "marriage medallion." As a jeweler, Louis designed his to depict the biblical story of Tobias and Sarah. It also noted their initials and the date of their marriage. When their vows were exchanged, the priest blessed the medallion and allowed Louis to give it to Zélie, along with her wedding ring.[182]

Following the ceremony, the couple took a train to Le Mans (roughly thirty-four miles away) to visit Zélie's sister in the convent. While most brides shed tears of joy on the day of their wedding, Zélie shed some tears of sadness while visiting her sister. Zélie still could not understand why she wasn't also called to religious life. But, over time, Zélie came never to regret marriage or children, for it was the life that God had chosen for her; it was the path for her and Louis to become saints, and it was their path of love. When Louis traveled on business trips, they would write letters to each other. Zélie's profound words sum up their love: "I kiss you with all my heart. I'm so happy today at the thought of seeing you again that I can't work. Your wife who loves you more than her life."[183]

Without Louis's mother's prayers and encouragement, he and Zélie might have remained single for the rest of their lives. But for this couple's desire to never settle for mediocrity or for less than a virtuous spouse, the world

---

[182] "Saints Louis and Zélie Martin, The Parents of Saint Thérèse of Lisieux," www.louisandzeliemartin.org/louis-and-zelies-marriage-meda.
[183] Martin and Martin, *A Call to a Deeper Love*, 52.

would have never known their daughter, Saint Thérèse of Lisieux, and her little way. Truly, the Martins answered the call to have "saintly succession" alive and well in the lineage of their family!

BERNARD AND ELLEN CASEY

Five years after Saints Louis and Zélie Martin entered the covenant of marriage, another couple would do so across the Atlantic Ocean: Bernard and Ellen Casey, who would become the parents of Blessed Solanus Casey. Connections can play a significant role in forming marriages. Besides physical attraction and virtue, which was seen in the Martins, some people are drawn to their spouse because they grew up in the same town, graduated from the same college, or shared the same nationality or religion. In the story of Tobit, Saint Raphael connected Tobias and Sarah, who were related. Bernard and Ellen Casey's shared nationality, virtue, and great love for their Catholic Faith brought them together in 1860. According to a biographer, Father Michael Crosby, "On July 4th, 1860, 'Barney' Casey met Ellen Murphy at a picnic in Biddeford, Maine. Her face 'beamed with kindness' in a way that attracted the serious Barney. After a short courtship, Barney proposed marriage. Ellen was sixteen."[184] Without a doubt, there was love at first sight. At the same time, Bernard had encountered virtue, which radiated through Ellen's countenance.

---

[184] *Blessed Solanus Casey: The Official Account of a Virtuous American Life*, ed. Michael Crosby, 14.

It was fitting that Solanus Casey's parents would meet somewhere simple like a picnic. After all, he joined the Capuchin order, which esteems simplicity and poverty. Both hailed from different parts of Ireland; Bernard grew up in County Monaghan while Ellen was born in County Armagh (now Northern Ireland). But the potato famine led both the Casey and Murphy families to emigrate to the United States. God's will can unfold anywhere, even in another country.

Falling in love can get complicated, especially when family gets involved. Three of Ellen's siblings had moved to Minnesota, which prompted her mother to follow suit (Ellen's father had died from the famine in Ireland). Unfortunately, Ellen's mother did not initially support her proposed marriage. Crosby declares,

> When Ellen wrote to her mother in Minnesota that Barney had asked her to marry him, Brigid Murphy— now helping to take care of Mary Ann's twins (Ellen's sister's children)—recalled that Mary Ann had married when she was sixteen. Consequently, her response was abrupt: Ellen was to leave Boston immediately and come to Hastings.
>
> When Ellen arrived her mother explained that she wanted her to enjoy the years of her youth before being saddled with family responsibilities. Brigid arranged that Ellen would live with Mrs. Ignatius Donnelly, whom she had befriended in the choir at Guardian Angels Church in Hastings. True to the pattern at that time, this was the "Irish church."

It stood a block from St. Boniface, the "German Church." After Ellen had spent three years with the Donnellys, Mrs. Donnelly convinced Brigid Murphy to let her daughter marry Barney Casey. Thus, when the Donnellys made a trip to Boston, Ellen accompanied them.[185]

The twenty-three-year-old Bernard Casey and nineteen-year-old Ellen Murphy married on October 6, 1863, in a church in Salem, Massachusetts. Their honeymoon lasted only a half-day, as Bernard's services as a shoemaker/repairer were needed for the Union soldiers during the Civil War.

The 1862 Homestead Act led Bernard and Ellen to resettle in Prescott, Wisconsin, on the Mississippi River, closer to family. Their sixth of their sixteen children, Bernard Francis Casey, named after his father, would honor his parents' name forever as he is currently (at the time of this writing) on the path to sainthood. Bernard the son became Blessed Solanus Casey, a humble Capuchin friar, who served as his monastery's doorkeeper for years. Many sought him for his counsel and his prayers for healing.

Interestingly, Bernard, like his father, proposed to a young girl. Her name was Rebecca Tobin, and she was sixteen at the time. Rebecca's mother also responded by sending her away, in her case to a boarding school some forty miles away.

While "the Divine Matchmaker" did not have a match for Bernard Francis Casey like his father, it is because

---

[185] Crosby, *Solanus Casey*, 14.

God wanted to be His spouse in religious life. Hence both Bernard Casey Sr. and Jr. had to wait on the Lord in their uncertainty. God often keeps us waiting to prepare us for something more or to teach us patience. Both father and son show us that true love is worth waiting for, while Ellen Casey shows us the beautiful example of obedience to one's parents. In the Caseys' lives, Saint Paul's words truly came to life, "We know that to them that love God, all things work together unto good, to such as, according to his purpose, are called to be saints" (Rom. 8:28).

SERVANTS OF GOD KAROL AND EMILIA WOJTYŁA

Just six years after Pope Saint John Paul II was canonized, the cause for his parents, Karol and Emilia Wojtyła, was opened in 2020. John Paul gave over one hundred lectures on human sexuality in a span of five years, referred to today as the "Theology of the Body."[186] Perhaps some people wonder how a celibate pope could know so much about God's plan for marriage and family life. But like most children raised in a holy environment, it was his parents who provided the first education concerning the splendor of marital love.

---

[186] This section uses several quotes from an unpublished English translation of the Polish edition: Milena Kindziuk, *Emilia and Karol Wojtyła: Parents of St. John Paul II* (Wydawnictwo Espirit, 2020). The Polish Edition is called *Emilia I Karol Wojtylowie: Rodzice sw. Jana Pawla II*. I would like to thank Roxanne Lum and Pawel Cetlinski for their assistance on this translation.

Karol Wojtyła Sr., the Pope's father, was born in Lipnik on July 18, 1879, to Maciej and his wife Anna (née Przeczek), the daughter of a baker. Anna died when Karol was a young boy. Karol's stepsister, Stefania, was born in 1891 of Maciej's second marriage to Maria Zalewska, the daughter of a tailor. Maciej Wojtyła died in Lipnik on September 23, 1923, when his grandson, the future pope, was not yet three and a half. The Wojtyła family hailed from southern Poland in the village of Czaniec near Kęt.[187] At the age of twenty-one, Karol became a noncommissioned officer in the 56th Infantry Regiment (Graf Daun Regiment) of the Austro-Hungarian army. After eighteen years of military service, he became an officer.

Emilia Anna Kaczorowska was born on March 26, 1884. Emilia's father, Feliks Kaczorowski,[188] was born in Biała on June 26, 1849, and worked as a saddler. In 1875, he married Maria Scholz, the third daughter of a cobbler. A year later the family moved to Kraków. Emilia is thought to have completed eight grades at a school run by the Sisters of Mercy.

But before the Wojtyłas could raise a saint, God led them together in a mysterious way—one which is still debated today. In her book, *Emilia and Karol Wojtyła: Parents of St. John Paul II*, Milena Kindziuk provides a few theories on how this holy couple met. According to tradition, Karol Wojtyła and Emilia Anna Kaczorowska met in one of Kraków's picturesque churches. The problem is

---

[187] Munk, *From the youth to the holiness [Od młodości, do świętości]*, 5.
[188] In Polish, the last name "Kaczorowski" ends in "i" for male family members, while it ends in "a" for female family members.

that no one in the family has corroborated that meeting. One speculation is that the couple met in Biała (present day Bielsko-Biała), where Emilia traveled as a young girl and later as an adult (this was her mother's hometown). Another theory is that Karol and Emilia met in Kraków, Emilia's birthplace. Providentially, nearly one hundred years to the day after his mother's birth on March 26, 1884, Pope Saint John Paul II knelt before a statue of his Heavenly Mother and consecrated the world to the Immaculate Heart of Mary. The Pope's motto was *Totus Tuus* or "Totally Yours," reflecting his personal love and devotion to Mary.

But back to Karol and Emilia's first encounter. As Kindziuk declares, "For sure Emilia must have been attracted to the military look of Karol, just like the old Polish saying: 'There's a line of women behind a military suit.' The engagement lasted close to one year before they got married on 10 February 1906."[189] If you look at Emilia's wedding picture, you'll notice she "has piercing eyes which catch the viewer's attention,"[190] not to mention her dignified appearance. Even more attractive was her cultured background, much like her son's. She grew up in a time of aesthetically beautiful churches and museums and the flourishing of Polish literature. She spoke Polish and German.

Emilia was likely attracted to Karol's strength. His military personnel file described him as "hair: dark blond, green eyes, proportional nose, oval face, height 171 cm,

---

[189] Kindziuk, *Emilia and Karol Wojtyła*, 16.
[190] Kindziuk, 29.

language: Polish, German, shoe size 14."[191] It is worth mentioning that Emilia grew up across from a cloistered convent of Felician nuns.[192] She would have likely prayed there and asked God to send her a holy man of prayer, a man who would understand and cherish the secret garden of her heart. Similar to nuns fleeing the world for a cloister, a married woman flees a world of men for one man, the one whom she seeks to give her heart to outside of Christ.

When the couple married, Karol was twenty-seven and Emilia twenty-one. Emilia knew the cross of suffering, having lost her own mother when she was thirteen, along with losing three siblings before her marriage. Emilia's loving father and later her stepmother helped prepare her for a happy marriage.

On February 10, 1906, Karol and Emilia were married in a large baroque church. According to Munk, "the wedding took place in Krakow, at the Garrison Church of the Holy Apostles Peter and Paul, the marriage was blessed by the chaplain Kazimierz Plachedko (a military chaplain). Jozef Kuczmierczyk and Feliks Kaczorowski were witnesses of this marriage."[193] Perhaps this was the place they first locked eyes after locking eyes on Him who gave His life for them. Today there is a plaque on the church that reads, "In this church Emilia nee Kaczorowska and NCO Karol Wojtyła, parents of St. John Paul II, received the Sacrament of Matrimony."[194]

---

[191] Kindziuk, 21.

[192] Kindziuk, 29.

[193] Munk, *From the youth to the holiness [Od młodości, do świętości]*, 5–6.

[194] Kindziuk, *Emilia and Karol Wojtyła*, 12.

Karol's stepsister[195] recounted the couple's wedding appearance: "Karol, as the groom, looked outstanding in his military outfit. In the wedding picture he is wearing a black uniform with three stars signifying his sergeant rank, he looked extremely elegant. He was not too tall, had a slim face with black moustache and looked serious as usual."[196] Emilia, on the other hand, was described as "a tall, twenty-one-year-old lady from Kraków, with dark eyes, beautiful hair in a bun, holding her husband's arm. She was wearing a long, white ruffled wedding dress and a veil decorated with the same flowers in the bouquet that she was holding. One can notice that she was wearing makeup—her face looks smooth and both her eyes and eyebrows are underlined."

It is popular for married couples to ride in a carriage following their wedding. But there is evidence that Karol and Emilia took a horse and carriage *to* their wedding, as Emilia's father repaired carriages for his occupation.[197] Nothing is mentioned concerning their reception or honeymoon, though the couple did make a visit to see Karol's family in Czaniec.[198]

The Wojtyłas were blessed with three children: Edmund, Olga, and Karol, who later became Pope Saint John Paul II. Sadly, Olga died sixteen hours after birth. Edmund, a doctor, died at the age of twenty-six from scarlet fever, which he contracted while helping a young patient. As Pope Saint John

---

[195] Karol Wojtyla Sr.'s mother died when he was two years old.
[196] Kindziuk, *Emilia and Karol Wojtyła*, 11.
[197] Kindziuk, 14.
[198] Kindziuk, 15.

Paul II once declared: "My brother Edmund died from scarlet fever in a virulent epidemic at the hospital where he was starting as a doctor. I was twelve. My mother's death made a deep impression on my memory and my brother's perhaps a still deeper one, because of the dramatic circumstances in which it occurred and because I was more mature."[199]

Karol Wojtyła, the third child of Karol and Emilia, was born on May 18, 1920. "Lolek, as family and friends would call him, was baptized by a military chaplain, Father Franciszek Zak, at St. Mary's Church on June 20, 1920, and formally given the names Karol Józef, which were reminiscent of the Habsburg monarchy his father had served."[200]

As Emilia's condition worsened, Karol Wojtyła Sr. did everything around the house: cooked, cleaned, shopped, and, above all, cared for his bride.[201] "In sickness and in health," one of the marriage promises says; this was lived to the fullest by Karol and Emilia. This holy couple witnessed more to the power of the sacrament of marriage in those difficult years than in their years of health and prosperity. In all this, Emilia kept her Faith and interior peace.[202] Here is a mother whose cross was literally her marriage bed because she was often bedridden. What a witness to the future saint!

One month before Pope Saint John Paul II's First Holy Communion, the forty-five-year-old Emilia Wojtyła passed away on April 13, 1929, with her husband next to her, after

---

[199] Frossard, "Be Not Afraid!," 14.
[200] Weigel, Witness to Hope, 27–28.
[201] Kindziuk, Emilia and Karol Wojtyła, 134.
[202] Kindziuk, 135.

receiving the Last Rites. The future pope was at school, his father and mother probably trying to shield their son from the suffering. Emilia's cause of death was listed as myocarditis, nephritis (or heart muscle inflammation and kidney inflammation).[203] When Karol Wojtyła brought his son home after Emilia died, the future John Paul II "approached his mother, kissed her cheek and started to cry."[204]

Karol Wojtyła Sr. likely never imagined that he would be raising an eight-year-old boy by himself. Unlike his father, Karol Wojtyła Sr. decided not to remarry, and simply lived a life of deep prayer. As Pope Saint John Paul II declared, "After my mother's death, his life became one of constant prayer. Sometimes I would wake up during the night and find my father on his knees, just as I would always see him kneeling in the parish church."[205]

At many weddings, it is natural to toast to the newlyweds, "For a lifetime of happiness and health." But this outcome is not always God's plan. God's blessings are often disguised in mysterious crosses, just as in mysterious courtships. Sometimes God interrupts a lifetime of earthly happiness in exchange for an eternal lifetime of happiness. Karol and Emilia were married for twenty-two years, and in that time their sacrificial love and suffering with joy was passed on to the boy who would become pope and influence a whole generation of Catholics.

Reflecting on his childhood, Pope Saint John Paul II once said, "I was not old enough to make my first communion

---

[203] Weigel, *Witness to Hope*, 29.
[204] Kindziuk, *Emilia and Karol Wojtyła*, 141.
[205] Pope John Paul II, *Gift and Mystery*, 20.

when I lost my mother, who did not have the happiness of seeing the day to which she looked forward as a great day. She wanted two sons, one a doctor and the other a priest; my brother was a doctor and, in spite of everything, I have become a priest."[206] Emilia's dreams came true for her in heaven.

You can tell a lot about a person by their possessions or lack thereof. Pope Saint John Paul II had only a few possessions when he died. One of his most prized possessions was a picture of his beloved parents that he kept in his bedroom. That photograph, which the pope saw daily, reminded him that sacrificial love and Faith must be at the heart of his vocation, for he too must lay down his life for his Bride, the Church, like his parents had done for one another. Pope Saint John Paul II was the icon of his parents' love. Whoever looked upon him saw Karol and Emilia shining through.

---

[206] Frossard, "*Be Not Afraid!*," 13.

CHAPTER 7

MARTYRED FOR LOVE

"I am not one to amuse myself with the heart of a lady, since my love is pure and noble. If I have waited until 20 years old to go out with a young lady, it is because I knew that I wanted to find real love. One must master his heart before he can give it to the one that is chosen for him by Christ."[207]

—Blessed Marcel Callo

MARRIAGE IS A hidden martyrdom, a daily dying to self. It is the school of sacrificial love and suffering. The crucible where a husband and wife learn to put their spouse and children before their own needs. The crucible where a husband and wife have no other will but God's will as they seek to please God and their spouse above everything. But, for some married souls, God calls them to the ultimate sacrifice: the offering of their very lives. No one ever imagines that God would choose them, their spouse, or even their fiancée to die for Christ. But sometimes God invites chosen souls to participate more fully in Calvary. With God's grace,

---

[207] "Blessed Marcel Callo," XV Ordinary General Assembly of the Synod of Bishops, secretariat.synod.va/content/synod2018/en/youth-testimonies/marcel-callo.html.

these individuals have prepared long before their courtship and marriage. Yes, "one must master his heart before he can give it to the one that is chosen for him by Christ." One must learn to die to himself daily before he can die for Christ or before he can sincerely love his spouse and children.

Christ's last recorded words in Saint John's Passion narrative were *Consummatum est*, "It is consummated" (John 19:30). No other translation save the Douay-Rheims version uses these striking words, words which connect Calvary and the marital act. A husband must look no further than Christ's passion and death to see the perfect example of how Christ loved His spouse, the Church. The bar has been raised and God expects nothing less than a daily martyrdom of the will. Most people will not be called to be a red martyr like those featured in this chapter, but they will be called to offer their lives daily, so that their spouse and children might have life. Let these saints who paid the ultimate sacrifice show us how.

SAINT THOMAS MORE, JANE COLT, AND ALICE MIDDLETON

Saint Thomas More's story is well documented. This sixteenth-century English lawyer, Lord Chancellor, and adviser to King Henry the VIII was martyred for refusing to acknowledge his friend and king as head of the Church of England and the king's annulment from his wife, Catherine of Aragon. A 1967 Hollywood movie was even made about More's heroic life, *A Man for All Seasons*. Lost in the most important details of his saintly life were his two happy marriages. Unlike Venerable Fulton Sheen's earlier analogy, More was not looking for the icing on the cake (physical beauty); he was more concerned with the cake, that is, with virtue. Make no mistake, one ought to be attracted to his or her spouse, but attraction is not the end of marriage. As referenced earlier, the Book of Proverbs reiterates this notion: "Favour is deceitful, and beauty is vain: the woman that feareth the Lord, she shall be praised" (Prov. 31:30).

James Monti, in his biography of Saint Thomas More, describes the saint's pursuit of his first wife in the following words:

> Thomas More considered the English countryside a far more wholesome place than the city, and thus when he had decided upon his state in life, he was ultimately to ask for the hand of a young and simple country girl in marriage. She was the oldest of three daughters of John Colt, a citizen of Netherhall in Essex, whom More visited sometime in 1504 or at the beginning of 1505. According to Crescare More (great-grandson of Thomas), all three of these young women were "very religiously inclined." William Roper tells us that at first More found the second of the girls the most attractive and "best favored," but when he considered that asking for her hand rather than for that of her older sister, Jane, would have deeply hurt the older girl, he, as Roper puts it, "of a certain pity framed his fancy" toward Jane and decided to marry her instead. In a poem that More translated into Latin from Greek only a few years

after his marriage, we find a description of what a man should look for in choosing a wife; we have no reason to doubt that in these words there is at least some reflection of the young Jane Colt:[208]

"And so, my friend, if you desire to marry, first observe what kind of parents the lady has. See to it that her mother is revered for the excellence of her character which is sucked in and expressed by her tender and impressionable little girl.

Next to this: what sort of personality she has: how agreeable she is. Let her maidenly countenance be calm and without severity. But let her modesty bring blushes to her cheeks . . . Let her glances be restrained; let her have no roving eye . . . Let her be either just finishing her education or ready to begin it immediately . . . Armed with this learning, she would not yield to pride in prosperity, nor to grief in distress—even though misfortune strike her down."[209]

Sadly, at the age of thirty-three, Thomas became a single father to four children under the age of six when Jane passed away unexpectedly. A month later, Thomas remarried Alice Middleton, a widow and seven years older than him. Alice had a few children, though all were grown except one. Thomas desired his children to have another mother, plus Alice was very well off. Historians believe

---

[208] Monti, *The King's Good Servant But God's First*, 47–48.
[209] "To Candidus: How to Choose a Wife," a poem no. 143, in CW 2/2, 185–87 quoted in Monti, *The King's Good Servant But God's First*, 48.

Thomas and Alice knew each other many years prior to their marriage, which explains their short engagement following Jane's passing. More than anything, Thomas was truly blessed to have fallen in love with two virtuous women. In fact, Thomas and Alice shared a great love for animals, including a pet monkey. One author, Susan Abernethy, said it best about his second wife:

> Alice was wise, the epitome of common sense, forthright in her speech and exercised practical efficiency. She demonstrated courage, sensibility, and frugalness. She could also be generous and warm hearted. She was just what Thomas needed at the time. She encouraged him to further his career. She took loving care of his four children plus Margaret Griggs (adopted girl) and her own daughter. She carefully supervised the children's education, assigning lessons and making sure they were completed. She is remembered as being fun loving by her grandchildren.[210]

When Saint Thomas More lost Jane, perhaps he thought his entire world was shattered. How am I to raise all these children by myself? How can I provide for them? Lord, I cannot do this by myself. These are common questions and sentiments any young widower or widow might ask when they lose their beloved, especially if they have little children. Sadly, many husbands and wives abandon God

---

[210] Susan Abernethy, "The Two Wives of Sir Thomas More," English Historical Fiction Authors, December 21, 2015, englishhistoryauthors .blogspot.com/2015/12/the-two-wives-of-sir-thomas-more.html.

when such tragedy occurs, even though God will never abandon them. God, the Divine Matchmaker, always provides, even when all hope seems lost, sometimes even in ways we never expect. Abernethy's words pertaining to More's second wife confirm this: "She (Alice) was just what Thomas needed at the time." In fact, Thomas and Alice planned to be buried in the same tomb as his first wife. Thomas wrote the epitaph seen in the Chelsea Old Church with the most striking words:

> Here lies Joanna (Jane), dear little wife of Thomas More, who intends this tomb for Alice and me. The first united to me in my youthful days, gave me a boy and three girls to call me father. The second, a rare distinction in a stepmother, was affectionate as if the children were her own. It is hard to say if the first lived with me more beloved than the second does now. Oh how blessed if fate and religion had permitted all three of us to live together. I pray the tomb and heaven may unite us, thus death could give what life could not give.[211]

Truly Jane and Alice represented the women described in Proverbs 31. They feared the Lord, and for that, Thomas thought they should be praised. When any couple exchanges vows, they have no idea how many years God will allow them to enjoy together on earth. The most important thing is to make the most of it, which Thomas, Jane, and Alice all did—living totally for God and trusting

---

[211] Abernethy, "The Two Wives of Sir Thomas More."

His will brings good out of evil, even out of death itself. While awaiting his impending martyrdom in the Tower of London, Thomas certainly had time to reflect on the many blessings God had bestowed on him throughout his life: the blessings of the Holy Eucharist, his own devout father, his children, and being doubly blessed to have been married to two virtuous women. Few men are blessed to be married to a saintly wife. Before ascending to the execution block, Saint Thomas More declared to the crowd, "I die the King's faithful servant, but God's first."[212] Perhaps he could have added, "I die Jane's and Alice's faithful husband," for he witnessed to the indissolubility of marriage, so much so, that he was willing to die for it.

BLESSED FRANZ AND FRANZISKA JÄGERSTÄTTER

One of the greatest mistakes biographers of the saints make is to paint a perfect picture of their lives. The following story is about second chances, because, in the words of the famed English author Oscar Wilde, "every saint has a past, and every sinner has a future."[213] Every person discerning marriage ought to strive to be pure and spotless for their future spouse. It was said that Christopher Columbus named the Virgin Islands after Saint Ursula and her 11,000 virgin martyrs. Certainly, Columbus made the

---

[212] Douglas O. Linder, "The Trial of Sir Thomas More: An Account," Famous Trials, https://famous-trials.com/thomasmore/986-home.
[213] Oscar Wilde, Goodreads, goodreads.com/quotes/12620-every -saint-has-a-past-and-every-sinner-has-a.

connection: there is something sacred and beautiful about a virgin, especially on the wedding night. Hence a bride's white wedding dress symbolizes purity. And yet, today, fewer women are virgins on their wedding day compared to ages past. Of course, the same sad fate applies to men. Even Saint Paul said about the Church, "That he (Christ) might present it to himself a glorious church, not having spot or wrinkle, or any such thing; but that it should be holy, and without blemish" (Eph. 5:27). Blessed Franz's courtship and life is a story of hope because God is a God of second chances. And it is a story about one woman taking a second chance on a future saint.

In the small village of Sankt Radegund, Austria, Franz was born to unwed parents in 1907. Some records indicate his parents were too poor to get married. Perhaps they didn't have enough money for a proper wedding and reception or to pay the dowry. Sadly, Franz's father died in World War I. His mother eventually met and married Heinrich Jägerstätter, who would adopt Franz.[214] The Jägerstätters attended Sunday Mass and raised Franz in a faith-filled environment. And yet, Franz led a wild and misspent life in his early twenties, rebelling against the Faith of his youth. At the time, he was the first person in his town to own a motorcycle. He allegedly fathered a daughter, Hildegard, with a local maidservant named Theresia Auer.[215]

---

[214] Zahn, *In Solitary Witness. The Life of and Death of Franz Jägerstätter*, 3.

[215] To this day, mystery surrounds whether Franz actually fathered Hildegard. Some of his closest friends deny such claims, but his wild youth also opens the possibility.

Franz agreed to pay child support. Later, he moved away for many years, perhaps embarrassed by the situation.

But something changed in his late twenties. He left behind his work in the iron ore industry, became a peasant farmer like his father, and returned home. The simplicity of farming and being near his loved ones certainly helped foster greater virtue. What led to his transformation? Some accounts believe it was meeting his future wife, Franziska, that helped bring Franz back to the Faith. She was a very devout Catholic, possibly even having discerned religious life. Other accounts believe that Franz already had an interior conversion before meeting Franziska, but that she helped assist with his reversion. It seems likely that Franz's illegitimate child and departure from his hometown reawakened Franz's Faith and allowed him to start over.[216] In fact, a priest, Father Karobath, expressed that Franz became interested in religious life himself following his conversion, but that he dissuaded Franz because he was set to run the family farm.[217] Many spiritual directors today tell recent converts or reverts, especially those who had been living in serious sin, to wait at least a year before applying to the seminary or religious life. The same would apply to entering the marriage state. The Divine Healer must heal the soul before it can truly be given away in love.

After his struggles with sin, Franz became even more convinced of the type of woman he wanted to marry, namely, a godly one. Franz was apparently a changed man,

---

[216] Zahn, *In Solitary Witness*, 39.
[217] Zahn, 38.

but would Franziska welcome such a man into her heart—a man who had not been pure? A man who used other women? A man who likely fathered a child? The details surrounding how and where Franziska met Franz are not clear. They likely met in the small town of Santk Radegund where they grew up. Today the population is less than one thousand people. Perhaps they met each other for the first time at their local Catholic parish. God's calling was right before their eyes, but the timing was critical. A godly man will be hard-pressed to find his wife if she is living in serious sin, and the same for a godly woman. Had Franz not wasted so many years, maybe he would have encountered Franziska earlier.

And yet, one thing is clear: Franziska gave Franz another opportunity to pursue a woman properly and purely. This time, Franz would pursue Franziska out of love, not lust, unlike his relationship with Theresia. To play off the words of Saint Maria Goretti's mother, who forgave the man who killed her daughter, Franziska could say to Franz, "If God loves you and forgives you from your past sins, how can I not do the same for you?"

Franz and Franziska were married on April 9, 1936, which happened to be Holy Thursday. They went to Rome for their honeymoon, where Pope Pius XI blessed the newly-married couple at a public audience. Together they had three daughters: Maria, Rosalia, and Aloisa. Franz embraced his wife's devotion. He would often pray the Rosary while plowing, and he sang hymns on the way to and from the Church, which he attended daily.[218] He also became the sexton of his local church.[219] Devotion to the Sacred Heart of Jesus, especially First Fridays, played a central role in their home life.[220]

Over time, Franz's religious zeal spilled over to his political zeal. Specifically, Franz was the only person in his village who opposed the Nazis. After refusing to join the army of the Third Reich, he was arrested and executed. In one of his farewell letters from prison, Franz said, "I can say from my own experience how painful life often is when one lives as a halfway Christian; it is more like vegetating than living."[221] He goes onto declare,

> Should it be that temptation is ever so strong that you feel you must give in to sin, give some thought to eternity. For it often happens that a man risks his temporal and eternal happiness for a few seconds of pleasure. No one can know whether he will ever again have an opportunity to confess or if God will give the grace to repent of his sin. Death can surprise us at any minute, and in an accident one very seldom has time enough to awaken repentance and sorrow. This much I can tell you from my own experience.[222]

---

[218] Zahn, 40.
[219] Church officer charged with the maintenance of the building like the sacristan of today.
[220] Zahn, *In Solitary Witness,* 83.
[221] Zahn, 33.
[222] Zahn, 34.

As a wild youth, Franz only thought about this passing earth. But through suffering and love, he knew that life was so much more than chasing pleasure. No, it was about striving for heaven, a place of never-ending joy. As Franz neared his final days before his martyrdom, he penned an inspiring letter to a teenager named Franz Huber. As the young boy's confirmation sponsor, Franz wanted to instill hope in him. Blessed Franz declared, "Even the most courageous and best Christians can and will fall but they will not lie for long in the filth of sin. Instead they will pull themselves together and draw new strength from the sacraments of Penance and Holy Communion and strive on to their goal. And should anxious days come upon us when we feel we are being crushed under the weight of our troubles, let us remember that God burdens none of us with a heavier cross than he can bear."[223]

With God's help and his wife's support, Franz strove never to let his dark past cast a shadow on his present life. He was a new man in Christ, forgiven and strengthened by the sacraments. While imprisoned for several months,[224] Franz penned the following letter to Franziska:

> Dearest wife, today it is seven years since we spoke our vows of love and fidelity before God and the priest, and I believe we have faithfully kept these vows to this day. I also believe that, even though we must now live apart, God will continue to give

---

[223] Zahn, 35.

[224] At first, Franziska opposed her husband's decision to contentiously object to the war, but she later came to support his decision.

us the grace to keep them until the end of our lives. When I look back upon all this joy and the many graces that have been mine for these seven years, it seems at times almost to border on the miraculous. If someone were to tell me that there is no God or that God does not love us—and if I were to believe him—I would not be able to explain how all this has come to me. Dearest wife, this is why, no matter how we may dread the future, He who has upheld us and given us joy till now will not abandon us then either. If only we do not forget to give thanks and do not hold ourselves back in our striving for heaven, God will permit our joy to continue on for all eternity.

Though I sit behind prison walls, I still believe I can build further on your love and devotion in days to come. And should I have to leave this life, I will still [rest easy in] my grave, for you know that I am not here as a criminal. It makes me very happy that you have had a Mass read for today, for I know you have given special thought to me while participating in it.[225]

Just as nothing can separate us from God's love, so nothing could separate a holy couple like Franz and Franziska from each other. Neither prison walls, nor their past sins, nor the threat of death could destroy Franz and Franziska's love, because it was rooted in the love of Christ. When Franziska visited her husband in prison, many thought she would convince Franz to change his mind and fall in

---

[225] Zahn, *In Solitary Witness*, 69–70.

line with the Nazis. She did not. Franz was convinced that fighting for the Nazis would be a serious sin and Franziska came to support him. Franz would boldly say, "I cannot believe that, just because a man has a wife and children, he is free to offend God by lying (not to mention all the other things he would be called upon to do)."[226]

In his final letter written to his wife and children, Blessed Franz asked his wife and children to pray for his soul, to keep the commandments, and "through God's grace we will soon meet again in heaven!"[227] He also wrote, "Dearest wife and mother! I thank you once more from my heart for everything that you have done for me in my lifetime, for all the love and sacrifice that you have borne for me: and I beg you again to forgive me if I have hurt or offended you, just as I have forgiven everything. . . . May God accept my life in reparation not only for my sins but for the sins of others as well."[228] Franz was shortly thereafter beheaded, bowing his head to almighty God alone.

During Franz's beatification ceremony at St. Mary's Cathedral in Linz, Austria, in 2007, his then ninety-four-year-old wife along with their three daughters and Franz's daughter from a previous relationship, Hildegard, were present to celebrate the sinner who now had a future in heaven. At the ceremony, Franziska kissed an urn containing a relic of her husband. Blessed Franz gave the ultimate sacrifice when he offered his life, but his wife may have made the greater sacrifice. She selflessly

---

[226] Zahn, 98.
[227] Zahn, 104.
[228] Zahn, 103.

allowed her husband to stay true to his Faith, resulting in her becoming a widow at the age of thirty after only seven years of marriage. Franziska raised three daughters by herself. The forgiveness, love, and mercy that Franziska showed to Franz enabled him to accept the same from God.[229]

Some people do not even get a chance to make a first impression because their reputation precedes them. During their courtship, Franziska likely heard gossip from the townspeople concerning Franz. Perhaps some whispered to her, "He is a disgrace," which could have ended the relationship had she listened. Later in life, many in the farming village blamed Franziska for her husband's "radical or fundamentalist views," which led to his martyrdom.[230] In all things, Franziska remained yoked to her husband. She could have pressured him to choose her and their children at the expense of going against his conscience, but she did not. Instead, she willed the best for him because she wanted God's will to be done. True love cannot grow without being tested by trials. How true was their love when they surrendered the one they loved most back to God.[231]

---

[229] "Franz Jägerstätter (1907–1943)," Vatican.va, vatican.va/news_ser vices/liturgy/saints/ns_lit_doc_20071026_jagerstatter_en.html.

[230] Tom Roberts, "Franz Jägerstätter's Widow, 'a warm, gentle soul,' dies at 100," National Catholic Reporter, ncronline.org/news/people /franz-j-gerst-tters-widow-warm-gentle-soul-dies-100.

[231] In 2019, Hollywood released an incredible movie called *A Hidden Life* directed by Terrence Malick and based on Blessed Franz Jägerstätter's life.

BLESSED MARCEL CALLO
AND MARGUERITE DERNIAUX

Not every courtship makes it to the altar. In God's providence, some relationships are not meant to be. Such was the case with the Blessed Marcel and Marguerite. As heartbreaking as it was for this couple, God had better plans for them. But before it ended in tragedy, it began so beautifully.

Born on December 6, 1921, in Rennes, France, Marcel was described as being a joyous child. One of nine children, Marcel seemed poised to follow the path of marriage and family life because of his parents' and siblings' examples of sacrificial love. From his youth, Marcel helped with household chores and took care of his younger siblings—such is the blessing of large families which enable children to mature and to sacrifice sooner.

At the age of thirteen, Marcel became an apprentice to a printer to help support his family. Because he was committed to a life of moral excellence and even borderline perfectionism, he avoided any coworker who used profanities and told impure jokes.[232] He was also intent upon living a well-balanced life. He had a great sense of humor and loved to play various sports and card games.[233]

But things were about to change for the worse when World War II began in 1939. In the midst of war, there was love and peace in Marcel's heart, for he met his future fiancée, Marguerite, at the age of twenty in 1941.

---

[232] "Blessed Marcel Callo," Savior.org, savior.org/saints/callo.htm.
[233] "Blessed Marcel Callo," Savior.org.

This beautiful couple met in a Catholic group called the Jeunesse Ouvrière Chrétienne (JOC), or Young Christian Workers. They allegedly met at one of the underground meetings that Marcel helped lead. As they say, the stars aligned perfectly. But in truth, God had led them to each other because both Marcel and Marguerite were seeking God's will, especially through a strong prayer life. Marcel once declared, "I must be punctual and regular in my daily work, but I must not neglect my prayers, and from time to time, must make visits in the church. By the Mass and by Communion, I must become more and more like Christ."[234]

He further declared, "We are often bad instruments in God's hands, because we have bad habits, bad inclinations. We become good instruments when we center our lives around Christ. . . . Every day, I must become, little by little, more like Christ."[235]

Marcel chose Marguerite long before they met. Or as he said earlier, "One must master his heart before he can give it to the one that is chosen for him by Christ."[236] Every time Marcel chose virtue over vice, that is, purity over impurity, he chose Marguerite. A few years before meeting Marguerite, Marcel made a pilgrimage to Lourdes, and after that he would often renew his Marian consecration. Our Lady was guiding Marcel's vocation. She also

---

[234] Meghan Baruzzini, "Blessed Marcel Callo," Guard of Honor of the Sacred Heart of Jesus, guardofhonor-usa.org/about-us/saintly-members/blessed_marcel_callo/.
[235] Baruzzini, "Blessed Marcel Callo."
[236] "Blessed Marcel Callo," Savior.org, savior.org/saints/callo.htm.

teaches her spiritual daughters like Marguerite to imitate her virtue while interceding that they, too, meet a spouse like Saint Joseph.

Blessed Marcel sums up the desire of every saintly courtship with the following words: "If I have waited until 20 years old to go out with a young lady, it is because I knew that I wanted to find real love."[237] Marcel and Marguerite knew that real love could only be found in Christ, in chastity and purity, for a man and woman do not give away just their love to each another. No, they give away Christ's love. Love that is willing to die for another and love that is unwilling to send their fiancé/fiancée to hell is rarely found today. Marcel and Marguerite desired true love, which was worth the wait.

According to one report, "It took him (Marcel) about one year to declare his love to Marguerite and an additional four months before they first kissed. After being engaged, they imposed a strict spiritual rule of life which included praying the same prayers and going to Mass and receiving the Eucharist as often as they could."[238]

But the love and peace that Marcel and Marguerite felt for each other was to be tested like never before as German soldiers began to occupy their town. Around March 1943, a bomb destroyed the neighboring city, leading Marcel and his friends to help find the survivors. Sadly, his sister Madeline was killed.

---

[237] "Blessed Marcel Callo," Savior.org.
[238] "Blessed Marcel Callo," Savior.org.

Marcel was then enlisted in a German airplane factory. Rather than flee his assignment and put his family in jeopardy, Marcel obeyed, especially since his older brother was about to be ordained a priest.[239] Furthermore, Marcel believed that God was calling him to bring Christ to the other workers. When Marcel bid Marguerite farewell, she told him that he would die a martyr's death, but he felt unworthy to die for Christ.[240]

While in Germany, Marcel struggled with deep depression. The conditions were harsh, and he missed his fiancée and family. Even worse, he was denied access to the sacraments for the first time. He wrote to Marguerite, "Finally Christ reacted. He made me understand that the depression was not good. I had to keep busy with my friends and then joy and relief would come back to me."[241] His mood was no doubt aided when he found a priest offering Sunday Mass. Strengthened by the Eucharist, Marcel began to lead others to Christ.

Marcel was eventually arrested by the Nazis at the age of twenty-three and then transferred to a concentration camp. They said he was "too Catholic" because he arranged for a Mass in the labor camps. A year later on March 19, 1945, Marcel died in the Mauthausen concentration camp in Austria from abuse and the horrid conditions. Throughout his imprisonment, he received the Holy

---

[239] Meghan Baruzzini, "Blessed Marcel Callo," Guard of Honor of the Sacred Heart of Jesus, guardofhonor-usa.org/about-us/saintly-members/blessed_marcel_callo/.

[240] Baruzzini, "Blessed Marcel Callo."

[241] "Blessed Marcel Callo," Savior.org, savior.org/saints/callo.htm.

Eucharist secretly. When he died, Marcel was twenty-four-years old, the same age as Saint Thérèse of Lisieux when she died. Like Thérèse, Marcel also died of tuberculosis, along with other ailments.

After Marcel passed away, Marguerite remained single for the rest of her life. Perhaps her heart could never love another man. She remained committed to the JOC group and worked as a postal clerk. Though Marcel was a martyr, Marguerite was also a martyr in spirit. She suffered in her soul the grief of losing the one whom she promised to spend her life with.

Marcel was beatified on March 4, 1987, by Pope Saint John Paul II. Blessed Marcel's feast day is March 19, the date of his death. He is the patron of youth workers and those struggling with depression. Marguerite died in 1997, fifty-two years after her one true love went to his eternal reward. Little is known about Marguerite's life. Even though she and Marcel's courtship was brief, it was holy. While they were never married on earth nor would be in heaven, Marcel went to prepare a place for his fiancée in the wedding feast of heaven where they would be united to Christ forever. And so, Marcel, at last, could finally have that first dance with Marguerite. Can you imagine the sight that greeted Marguerite at the moment of her death? Certainly, Marcel would have come for Marguerite and helped escort her to God.

Servants of God Cyprien and Daphrose Rugumba

In 2015, Cyprien and Daphrose Rugumba's cause for beatification was opened. Prior to their marriage, this Rwandan couple sincerely sought to follow God's will. They wanted to follow the vocation God wanted for them, not simply the one they wanted. This was the first step to their becoming saints, for those who seek the will of God will eventually find it.

Despite being born in the same village of Cynaika in southern Rwanda, they found each other later in life. Cyprien was born in 1935, Daphrose in 1944. Cyprien attended minor and major seminary before meeting Daphrose. But he left because of the various scandals at the seminary and various unorthodox professors attacking the Catholic Faith. The door closed not only on the priesthood, but, sadly, on Christ and His Church—disillusioned by his seminary experiences, Cyprien abandoned his Catholic Faith. And yet, God never closes the door on anyone.

Cyprien pursued a secular career, finding his calling as a poet, author, composer, and eventually a prominent government official, where he sought to promote and safeguard Rwanda's traditional art.[242] He pursued several other women before falling in love with a lady named Xaverina. They were engaged after a short courtship. But like the

---

[242] "Killed in Rwandan genocide, this couple is being considered for sainthood," Catholic News Agency, catholicnewsagency.com /news/40992/killed-in-the-rwandan-genocide-this-couple-is-being -considered-for-sainthood.

seminary, God closed another door in Cyprien's life, one even more tragic than the seminary, when his fiancée was killed in 1963. The circumstances surrounding her death remain unknown, but were likely related to the future ethnic wars. At this point, it is not certain whether Cyprien was practicing his Catholic Faith. But one thing is for sure: Cyprien's trust in a loving God was once again put to the test. He had become a modern-day version of Job, though without the same staunch Faith.

Because of Cyprien's great love for his late fiancée and her family, he asked to marry her cousin, Daphrose, a pious Catholic.[243] Daphrose was a teacher. Her heart felt compassion for the widower. Perhaps she wondered whether she could love Cyprien as her late cousin did, or whether Cyprien could love again. Just as every person is unique, so too are every engagement and marriage. When a fiancé or spouse dies, the longing to be with him or her never goes away.

Little is known about Cyprien and Daphrose's courtship. But they were married in 1965. At the time, Cyprien was around thirty years old, while Daphrose was twenty-one. At one point during their marriage, the couple was separated for eight months.[244] The reason for the separation was disturbing: Cyprien's family believed that Daphrose dabbled in the occult, and therefore, they advised him to disown his wife. Cyprien's family came to this unfounded conclu-

---

sion when the couple's second child was born healthy, after the death of their first child from a miscarriage. Following his family's ill-advised counsel, Cyprien sent his wife away while he kept the child.[245] Cyprien later realized his mistake, and his wife returned after eight months.

After the couple got back together, Cyprien cheated on Daphrose, even fathering a child out of wedlock. Daphrose's piety and love for the Catholic Church pricked Cyprien's conscience, yet he criticized her Faith to deflect his own culpability in their conflict.[246] It seemed as if the couple was no longer one flesh, but two, at war with one another.

Daphrose remained resolute in her vows, intensifying her prayers for Cyprien's conversion. Even if Cyprien would not join her at Mass, she was determined to bring their children with her each Sunday and raise them in the Faith. The couple went on to have ten children. After seventeen long years of persevering prayer (the same amount of time that Saint Monica prayed for Saint Augustine's conversion), God heard Daphrose's plea, but not in the way she expected. In 1982, Cyprien faced a near fatal illness that would lead to his reversion to the Faith and the rejuvenation of his marriage.[247] Prior to this unexpected blessing in disguise, Cyprien and Daphrose's marriage had withered for years, even reaching the brink of divorce.

[245] Meg Hunter-Kilmer, "Saints who struggled with their in-laws," Aleteia, aleteia.org/2021/05/22/saints-who-struggled-with-their-in-laws/.
[246] Hunter-Kilmer, "Saints who struggled with their in-laws."
[247] "Killed in Rwandan genocide, this couple is being considered for sainthood," Catholic News Agency, catholicnewsagency.com/news/40992/killed-in-the-rwandan-genocide-this-couple-is-being-considered-for-sainthood.

But Daphrose kept knocking with persistence until God opened the door.

Cyprien became a changed man—one of humility and joy—through the prayers of his wife.[248] He pleaded for her forgiveness and she freely gave it. God revitalized their failing marriage with His grace. In 1989, the couple went on a life-changing pilgrimage to France to see where Jesus appeared to Saint Margaret Mary. During their pilgrimage they also encountered the Emmanuel Community, a Catholic association of the faithful rooted in the Charismatic renewal, a group that would greatly shape the couple's prayer life.

God's grace would prepare them for the future. As racial hatred began to spread between the ethnic groups of the Hutus and Tutsis, Rwanda became immersed in a civil war. On April 7, 1994, after spending the night in Eucharistic Adoration, Cyprien and Daphrose were murdered at home alongside six of their ten children. This holy couple refused to allow hatred to control their hearts and so they were targeted. Tragically, close to a million people died in the genocide.

Many couples dream of growing old together and watching their children and grandchildren live meaningful lives. But God led this holy couple on a different path, one filled with suffering, sorrow, and martyrdom. In the end, it was not their pain that defined them but the joy that emanated from their trials. God invites every couple to help carry His cross,

---

[248] "Killed in the Rwandan genocide, this couple is being considered for sainthood," Catholic News Agency.

but not every couple responds wholeheartedly. Cyprien and Daphrose remind us that the cross is the intersection where every road must meet in order to reach heaven.

SAINT GIANNA AND PIETRO MOLLA

Canonized on May 16, 2004, Saint Gianna Beretta Molla was diagnosed with a huge fibromyoma (a benign tumor) in her uterus near the end of the second month of her last pregnancy. She was free to choose and decide among three different solutions: to have a hysterectomy (the safest solution for her life), to remove the fibromyoma with a surgery and put an end to that pregnancy with an abortion, to remove only the tumor and continue with the pregnancy. (This last was the riskiest solution for her life. The risk was this: the surgery necessary to remove the fibromyoma would have left a scar that could rupture during the pregnancy, causing a rupture to the uterus as well, with mortal risk for her and for the baby.) She chose the latter, and her daughter, Gianna Emanuela, was born by C-section because the natural childbirth did not work. Saint Gianna suffered terrible abdominal pains caused by septic peritonitis, a complication of delivery, and, despite all the treatments, she died seven days after giving birth. Saint Gianna was the antithesis of the radical feminist movement because she valued her preborn child more than her own life.

Few people know that Saint Gianna almost did not get married. Prior to her marriage and for a long time, she considered following her brother Father Alberto—a physician missionary, who became a Capuchin friar in Grajaú, Brazil—as a lay missionary. She asked her relatives to join her in praying novenas for clarity in her vocation. Her daughter Gianna Emanuela describes her mother's beautiful search for God's will:

> At the same time, while praying a great deal and asking for prayers from others, she was wondering about what her vocation could be, which she considered a gift from God as well; for this reason, she worried about knowing God's will for her, to be able to serve Him in the best way. She was not in a hurry: she went on to pray until she was sure of the vocation to which the Lord was calling her.
>
> At first, she thought she could be a lay missionary in Brazil, to help her brother, Father Alberto, as a physician. But her body was not strong enough to bear the equatorial heat, and her Spiritual Director was able to convince her that her vocation was different—otherwise the Lord would have given her the health necessary (to go to Brazil); he encouraged her to form a holy family herself too, like her original family had been, while imitating the example of her parents.
>
> In June 1954, at the age of almost 32, she went to Lourdes . . . because she wished to pray to Our Lady of Lourdes to let her meet the man who would be her spouse, the man that the Lord had prepared for her since eternity.[249]

---

[249] Gianna Emanuela Molla, *Witness of Gianna Emanuela Molla* to

Saint Gianna had a great love for Our Lady as she prayed the Rosary daily from her childhood. Like the best of mothers, Our Lady—venerated in Lourdes as the Immaculate Conception—interceded before God for Gianna. Shortly thereafter, Gianna felt a clear calling from the Lord to the vocation of marriage.

On the feast of the Immaculate Conception in December of 1954, she became better acquainted with Pietro Molla, her future spouse. Interestingly, her spiritual director never swayed her in one direction or another, but he did say these beautiful words: "If all good Catholic girls went into the convent, then where would we get our Christian mothers?"[250]

Like Saint Zélie, Saint Gianna benefited from an interior light. We should not seek or expect God to give us a sign when it comes to our vocation. Sometimes God's will is clear, but in most cases it is not as obvious. At times we must exercise the virtue of faith. Just as a small tree becomes a large tree through much watering and fertile soil, so too did Gianna's vocation unfold through much prayer and discernment. Prayer, but especially seeking God's will, is the key that unlocks the door to our vocation. As Gianna once wrote in her personal notes:

Patrick O'Hearn, August 25, 2022. She mentioned the testimony of her mother's youngest sister, Mother Virginia, a physician and Canossian Sister. Her mother made this confidence to Mother Virginia before going in pilgrimage to Lourdes.

[250] Holböck, *Married Saints and Blesseds Through the Centuries*, 457–58.

All things have a particular purpose. They all obey a law. Everything develops for a predetermined end. To each one of us, too, God has assigned a path, a vocation, and, besides physical life, the life of grace. Our earthly and eternal happiness depends on following our vocation well. What is a vocation? It is a gift from God: therefore it comes from God! If the gift is from God, our concern must be to know the will of God. We must set out on that path: if God wills, never forcing the door, when God wills, as God wills.[251]

Yes, Gianna never forced her vocation; rather, she waited upon her Heavenly Father and Our Lady to offer it to her as a gift.

Gianna Emanuela also describes her father's great desire to have his own family:

I can say that, on the one hand, together with his great faith which permeated and strengthened every single aspect of his life, my Dad had a great devotion to work—he worked very much, too much! Then, only my Mom was able to save him a little bit from all this work, bringing him to the Concerts of classical music, and to take mountain trips! and a great affection for his parents and his sisters; on the other hand, he felt the Lord was calling him to the vocation of marriage, and he had a great desire to have

---

[251] Pelucchi, *St. Gianna*, 128.

his own family. He was praying a great deal to Our Lady to let him meet "*A holy mother for his children.*"

The Lord was really calling my parents to the vocation of marriage just as they thought, because the Virgin Mary had heard their prayers. And so, thanks to Her, their wonderful hearts and souls could meet at last, because they already knew each other five years before this![252]

Pietro once reflected on their initial meetings and subsequent courtship and marriage, reflections that ended up being submitted for Gianna's beatification:

I met you for the first time in my life at your brother Ferdinando's doctor's office in September 1949. I had gone to Ferdinando because I was sick. We said hello and hardly looked at each other. My first impression of you was of an extremely direct, serious person. I saw you for the second time the following year on April 16 at the Magenta Hospital, again in a white gown. You had just finished giving a blood transfusion to my sister Teresina, whom the Lord called to be among his angels a few days later. Again in that extremely painful situation, our glances hardly met.[253]

Pietro described other encounters with Gianna after she opened a doctor's office in Mesero, his birthplace; and he

---

[252] Gianna Emanuela Molla, *Witness of Gianna Emanuela Molla* to Patrick O'Hearn, August 25, 2022.
[253] Molla, *Saint Gianna Molla*, 117.

testified her patients held her in the highest esteem. He noted, "From the second half of 1950 to November 1954, we had some brief encounters, rapid exchanges of greetings and a half smile on the occasion of your visits to the nurse or your trips from Magenta to Mesero and mine from Mesero to Magenta."[254] But it was not until December 8, 1954, that they officially met at Father Lino Garavaglia's first Mass, who later became the Bishop of Cesena. In his diary, Pietro vividly recalled that day: "I recall you while you congratulated Father Lino and his relatives with your kind, broad, good smile. I recall how you devoutly made the sign of the cross before the meal. I also recall you in prayer at the Eucharistic blessing. I still feel your cordial handshake, and I see again the sweet, luminous smile that accompanied it."[255]

In an interview with Elio Guerriero, Pietro described how this acquaintance turned into love: "Talking with Gianna, my good first impression was confirmed quickly. I found her an extraordinarily transparent person, extraordinarily gracious. Her looks, her attitude, her eyes, her beauty made her very attractive. I understood that she was right for me, that I would like to be with her. So, I had fallen in love, but I did not find words to express my feelings. Thank God, Gianna was more effusive, more open. By contrast, my temperament was more reserved because of my upbringing and life experiences."[256]

---

[254] Molla, 118.
[255] Molla, 119.
[256] Molla, 54.

Pietro was impressed by Gianna's beauty, her joyful countenance, and her reverence. What is fascinating about this couple is that they lived only a few miles apart and saw each other on several occasions, but never carried out a conversation until some five years later.

Pietro was also "extremely reserved and shy"[257] according to his daughter. At the same time, both Gianna and Pietro were focused on their work—Gianna as a pediatrician and Pietro as an engineer, which included long travels. These work demands made it difficult for them to find a spouse.

But something happened on December 8, 1954, the very day that Gianna finished her novena. According to the author Elio Guerriero, who edited all the letters of Gianna and Pietro:

> Suddenly it seemed as if a veil had fallen and each discovered the wonder and beauty of the other, the harmony of their ideals (love of family, of children, of those around them) that had been cultivated yet hidden from indiscreet eyes. Gianna was a beautiful woman, and Pietro quickly fell in love. She fascinated Pietro to the extent that she was able to draw him out of the isolation and workaholism that threatened to engulf him. On his part, Pietro gave a sense of security to the young woman who had already lost her parents some years before.[258]

---

[257] Gianna Emanuela Molla, *Witness of Gianna Emanuela Molla* to Patrick O'Hearn, August 25, 2022.
[258] Beretta, *The Journey of Our Love*, 16.

It is important for young men and women to pay attention to the people God places in their path. In many cases, it might not be love at first sight, but love can grow. Like Gianna and Pietro, we must always remain attentive to God's will. Not only was their love pure and holy but it was also truly romantic. In effect, Gianna reveals that it is possible to love a man and still love God completely. Gianna and Pietro's love letters during their courtship, their engagement, and marriage reveal a love that participates and mirrors God's inner life. Sadly, most young people today have never written a love letter. It is a lost art. This stems from several factors, including technological advances and the loss of chastity in our culture today. The thrill of pursuing a woman is largely unknown to men because man no longer finds the chase exhilarating and the woman no longer seeks to be pursued.

Gianna, more open than Pietro, was the first to declare her love—unusual, especially in those times—only two and a half months after the Feast of the Immaculate Conception when they first officially met. In her very first letter, on February 21, 1955, she wrote the following:

> Dearest Pietro,
>
> I hope you don't mind if I begin this letter by calling you by your first name and using such familiar language. After sharing our thoughts so openly yesterday, I think we can assume this level of intimacy, which will help us to understand and to love each other more and more.

I really want to make you happy and be what you desire: good, understanding, and ready for the sacrifices that life will require of us. I haven't told you yet that I have always been very sensitive and eager for affection. While I had my parents, their love was enough for me. Then, although remaining very united to the Lord and working for him, I felt the need for a mother, and I found her in the dear nun whom I told you yesterday.

Now there is you, whom I already love, and to whom I intend to give myself to form a truly Christian family.

Ciao, dear Pietro. Pardon my familiarity, but that's how I am. *Arrivederci*.

With affection, Gianna.[259]

The following day, Pietro wrote to Gianna:

My dearest Gianna,

I've read your letter over and over, and kissed it.

A new life is beginning for me: the life of your great (and greatly desired) affection and of your radiant goodness. We are starting the journey of our love.

I love you, my dearest Gianna.

I could not have received a greater or more ardently desired grace from our Heavenly Mother, Our Lady of Good Counsel, as she is invoked in my little church in Ponte Nuovo.

---

[259] Beretta, *The Journey of Our Love*, 48.

I so wanted and needed love and a family of my own. Now I have you, your love and affection, and I am happy.

My love is yours, and I want to raise a family with you. I too want to make you happy and understand you well.

Forgive me for not beginning a closer confidence sooner than I did. Thank you for your help and trust. With all my love, Pietro.[260]

This devout couple was engaged on April 11, 1955. Their engagement was a blessed time according to their daughter, Gianna Emanuela:

> They lived their engagement time as "a time of grace," with great joy and deep gratitude to the Lord and to the Virgin Mary as they prayed to them for their future family every day more and more. They were ready to face life's sorrows, too. On 5th July 1955, Mom wrote to Dad: "My dearest Pietro . . . It's true, there will be sorrows, too, but if we always love each other as we do now, then, with God's help, we'll know how to bear them together. Don't you think so? For now, though, let's enjoy the happiness of loving each other. I was always told that the secret of happiness is to live moment by moment and to thank the Lord for all that He, in his goodness, sends to us day after day."[261]

---

[260] Beretta, 49.

[261] Gianna Emanuela Molla, *Witness of Gianna Emanuela Molla* to Patrick O'Hearn, August 25, 2022.

On September 4, 1955, three weeks before their wedding on September 24, the Feast of Our Lady of Mercy, the almost thirty-three-year-old Gianna wrote these striking words to her forty-three-year-old fiancée, "In only twenty days, I'll be . . . Gianna Molla! What would you say about our making a triduum to prepare spiritually to receive this Sacrament? Holy Mass and Holy Communion on the twenty-first, twenty-second, and twenty-third, you at Ponte Nuovo, I at the Shrine of the Assumption. The Blessed Mother will unite our prayers and, because strength is found in unity, Jesus can't help but listen to us and answer our prayers. I'm sure you will say yes, and I thank you."[262]

The purity of their love and devotion to God was also evident in Pietro's letter written six days later on September 10, which touched Saint Gianna's heart. Pietro wrote:

> Dearest Gianna . . . you and I have undertaken our new life with the certainty that God wanted us together. These months have all been a crescendo of understanding and affection. Now we understand each other perfectly, because Heaven is our light and the Divine Law our guide . . . Now our love is full because we are one heart and soul, one feeling and love, because our love, strong and pure, knows how to wait for the blessing of Heaven. . . .[263]

---

[262] Beretta, *The Journey of Our Love*, 68.
[263] Gianna Emanuela Molla, *Witness of Gianna Emanuela Molla* to Patrick O'Hearn, August 25, 2022.

Gianna was intent upon selecting the best material for her wedding dress. She said to her sister, "Do you know, I want to choose a very beautiful fabric because later on I want to make a chasuble out of it, for the first Mass of any one of my sons who may become a priest."[264] On the eve of their wedding, Pietro gave Gianna a gold watch and a pearl necklace with a love note: "Gianna, May these [pearls] crown the wonder and purity of your beauty and virtue on our wedding day, in order that the one gift [a watch] may always mark the most beautiful and serene time of our lives, and that the other, the pearl necklace, signify the enchanting light of our love, your Mamma and mine, with a mother's love, give you these gifts, as do I, with the greatest love. Your Pietro."[265]

According to their daughter Gianna Emanuela,

> They got married in Magenta, on 24th September 1955, in the Basilica of Saint Martin, Mom's Parish Church, where she was baptized too. They settled in Ponte Nuovo of Magenta. Dad used to tell me that, because of his shy and reserved character, he would have preferred to get married in a small, secluded Church in the mountain, in the presence of few persons. He made the really great sacrifice to get married in this big Basilica with pleasure, to please his Gianna. . . .
>
> Along with their conjugal and family life, my parents made concrete and brought to fruition all the

---

[264] Brown, *No Greater Love*, 20.
[265] Beretta, *The Journey of Our Love*, 82.

aspirations, desires, and promises of their time of engagement, always living in God's grace, with His blessing and continuously doing His holy will. They always lived their love in the light of faith, and this is very clear reading their magnificent letters, in which the Lord and the Virgin Mary are always present.

There are many aspects of my parents' marriage that profoundly enlighten me and move me including their deep faith and unwavering confidence in Divine Providence, their deep humility—I think that humility is the fundamental virtue to become a saint, and the indispensable virtue for having all the other virtues—and their infinite mutual love, which made them more serene and stronger. I am also deeply touched by their immeasurable love for us, the children, and their family, their great mutual esteem, their reciprocal continuous communication and support, their intense and constant prayers of gratitude to the Lord and the Virgin Mary, and their love and charity towards their neighbors. They truly lived the Sacrament of Marriage as a vocation and as a path towards holiness.[266]

Gianna and Pietro's love for one another intensified the closer they drew to God. They allowed His love, along with Our Lady's intercession, to unite them. One of the most salient lessons Gianna and Pietro reveal is that spouses ought not just to fall in love once, but every day of their lives. Just as the Bridegroom, our Eucharistic Lord, pursues

---

[266] Gianna Emanuela Molla, *Witness of Gianna Emanuela Molla.*

His bride, the Church, at every moment of our lives, so too must the groom pursue his bride. Due to his frequent work travels, Pietro and Gianna would often write short love letters throughout their marriage. In fact, according to their daughter Gianna Emanuela, her parents wrote a letter to each other nearly every day during Pietro's visit to the United States from April 26 to June 16, 1959.[267]

Pietro's letter written on January 25, 1961, five years after his marriage, testifies to a human love that mirrors the Divine love. Pietro declared,

> My most beloved Gianna,
>
> I'm at the Hotel Des Indes, on the second floor, in a room just like the one we had in December for those wonderful nights of kisses and ineffable caresses and sweetest love.
>
> You are truly my full and perfect joy, most beloved and my most loving little wife!
>
> I think of you, at this moment sleeping so sweetly next to our marvelous treasures: such a diligent, caring, and untiring little mother.
>
> And I thank the Lord once more for the incomparable gift he gave me and for the ineffable joys he grants to us and to our family.
>
> Most lovingly, I kiss our children and I kiss and embrace you just as you kiss me and most sweetly press me to your heart.
>
> Your Pietro.[268]

---

[267] Gianna Emanuela Molla, *Witness of Gianna Emanuela Molla.*
[268] Beretta, *The Journey of Our Love*, 265.

When Pietro recalled those "wonderful nights of kisses and ineffable caresses and sweetest love," he was testifying to a love indicative of the Canticle of Canticles.[269]

What made their love so special was that both Gianna and Pietro never loved anyone else, as Gianna Emanuela stated:

> My Dad was a man of great purity. My Mom is the only woman in my Dad's life! He never kissed another woman except my Mom! I know that many women wished to marry my Dad, but he kept praying to Our Lady to let him meet *a holy mother for his children.* He waited forty-two years for the holy mother for his children!!! My Mom too was a woman of great purity. Her youngest sister and my aunt, Mother Virginia, told me that my Mom turned down many marriage proposals she received from men she never frequented; that Mom was considering to go to Brazil more than the marriage, and continued praying.[270]

Hence, the happiest and most intimate marriages are built upon the foundation of purity and chastity and, above all, on God Himself.

---

[269] A 1992 University of Chicago National Health and Social Life study along with other studies led the Family Research Council to conclude that devout Catholics have the best conjugal union of any demographic. In fact, compared to non-Catholics, Catholics consummate their vows more frequently. The studies also found a clear correlation between those who worship God weekly and marital intimacy.

[270] Gianna Emanuela Molla, *Witness of Gianna Emanuela Molla.*

Because of their great intimacy and openness to life, God blessed Gianna and Pietro with four children on earth and two in heaven. Sadly, Gianna suffered two miscarriages between her third and sixth child. Most fairy tales end with the predictable words, "And they lived happily ever after." With Gianna's premature death, their love story did not mimic the fairy tales. But they would live happily ever after in heaven, which ought to be the goal of every marriage.

Gianna died on April 28, 1962, at the age of thirty-nine. As her daughter Gianna Emanuela relates, "She wanted to receive Holy Communion, at least on her lips, also on Thursday and Friday, when she was no longer able to swallow the Holy Particle. On April 28, 1962, Saturday in Albis, at dawn, she was taken back to her family home in Ponte Nuovo, as she wished and had asked of my Papa previously. She died in her nuptial bed, where she gave birth to my siblings, at 8 a.m."[271]

Saint Gianna was a pro-life "white" martyr, saving her child at the risk of her own life. Pietro, for his part, accepted Gianna's decision; he, too, sacrificed himself for his children in Gianna's absence with the same love that they had shared, which was ultimately Christ's love. The greatest love of a mother is to lay down her life for her child as Gianna did for her daughter (see John 15:13). How beautiful that Saint Gianna died in her "nuptial bed," for marriage is a participation in Christ's passion, death, and resurrection.

---

[271] Gianna Emanuela Molla, *Witness of Gianna Emanuela Molla.*

Just as Gianna and Pietro surrendered to God's will when they fell in love, so now Pietro had to make an even greater act of surrender after God called his bride to Himself. Only two years later, his daughter Mariolina passed from this life at the tender age of six. As their daughter Gianna Emanuela recounts,

> I remember that my Dad told me he implored the Lord to save not only my life, but my Mom's life as well; the Lord, with His infinite wisdom and His impenetrable designs, did not intervene to save my Mom's life. My Dad, though with a profound sorrow, accepted His holy will, without understanding it.
>
> Only many years later he understood what the Lord wished for Mom, when the Church asked him the permission to open her Cause of Beatification, and Mom has been proclaimed "Blessed," as "Mother of a Family," on April 24, 1994, only 32 years after she died, by Saint John Paul II, and 10 years later, on May 16, 2004, "Saint" by the same Pope. "If she had remained here with us," Dad told me, "she would have kept on doing good to her family, her neighbor and her patients, but the Lord wished that Mom would do good to many, many more persons, and in so many parts of the world."
>
> A few months after my Mom entered Heaven, my Papa wrote a long letter addressed to my uncle, Father Alberto, his brother-in-law, of whom my Father was very fond, who lived in Brazil. This letter ends with this wonderful prayer: ". . . *And you,*

Gianna, help me to carry my Cross, day after day, and to realize God's will in a heroic way. That you may obtain the divine grace for our children and for me to become saints also. Grant that every day may bring us nearer to you and that every day we may ascend a step of Jacob's mystical ladder, at the top of which you are waiting for us. And grant that when God will call us as well He can find us worthy to come near, near, near to you forever. Amen."

I lived forty-eight years of my life with my Dad and I can testify that Mom answered my Dad's prayer: she helped him to carry his cross, day after day, and to realize God's will in a heroic way; and when the Lord called him to Himself as well, he was most worthy to live with her forever!

According to His will, my parents lived their conjugal and family life together for only six and a half years, then Mom entered Paradise. During the forty-eight years that Dad lived without her visible presence, they went on to be *"one heart and soul,"* very spiritually united and in communion with each other. True love, that is the love which lasts forever, is really much stronger than death!

I remember that Dad prayed a great deal and continued thanking the Lord, for everything. I was surprised that, even though he had suffered tremendously during his long life, he always told me: *"Eternity will not be enough for me to thank the Lord for all the graces He granted me during my long life,"* referring, in particular, to the grace that he could be present in St. Peter Square in Rome at my Mom's proclamation as a "Saint" by Pope Saint John Paul II. . . .

Every morning when I wake up and open my eyes, after having thanked God for the gift of life, I pray to the Lord, to the Virgin Mary and to Saint Joseph to help me to be the least unworthy as possible of my holy parents. I am living with the joy and the hope of being able to embrace them again, together with Mariolina and all my other loved ones, one day, and, this time, forever, to never leave each other again![272]

Love and death will always remain a great mystery. To love is to die to oneself and to die for another is the greatest act of love.

---

[272] Gianna Emanuela Molla, *Witness of Gianna Emanuela Molla.*

CHAPTER 8

COURTSHIPS THAT
TRANSFORMED
THE CHURCH

*"Dear families, today we have distinctive confirmation that
the path of holiness lived together as a couple is possible,
beautiful, extraordinarily fruitful, and fundamental for
the good of the family, the Church and society."*[273]

—Pope Saint John Paul II

EVERY COURTSHIP AND marriage is meant to set the world
and Church ablaze with Christ's love. God wants marriage to be a vehicle to bring as many souls as possible to
heaven. Just as God saved the human family through the
Holy Family, He wants to bring Christ into our families
and so redeem mankind. Far from being some private
matter between two people, marriage has a missionary nature. A couple's children will be sent out into the

---

[273] Pope Saint John Paul II, "Beatification of the Servants of God Luigi
Beltrame Quattrocchi and Maria Corisini, Married Couple," Vatican.
va, vatican.va/content/john-paul-ii/en/homilies/2001/documents/hf
_jp-ii_hom_20011021_beltrame-quattrocchi.html.

world to spread the Gospel. One holy marriage can impact countless generations just as one dysfunctional marriage can harm several generations. We need only read the lives of the people who caused our world and Church the most damage and you will see a pattern: sin begets sin, goodness begets goodness.

Pope Saint John Paul II delivered the epigraph used for this chapter at the occasion of Luigi and Maria Quattrocchi's beatification Mass on October 21, 2001. The Holy Father's words hearken back to Jesus's words: "By their fruits you shall know them. Do men gather grapes of thorns, or figs of thistles? Even so every good tree bringeth forth good fruit, and the evil tree bringeth forth evil fruit. A good tree cannot bring forth evil fruit, neither can an evil tree bring forth good fruit. Every tree that bringeth not forth good fruit, shall be cut down, and shall be cast into the fire. Wherefore by their fruits you shall know them" (Matt. 7:16–20). The fruits of a holy marriage often produce vocations to the priesthood, religious life, and holy marriages. Therefore, a person need not become a missionary or join a convent to transform the Church and the world. Rather, God calls most souls to enter marriage where they will impact generation upon generation by handing down the mustard seed of faith. The domestic Church, if lived to the fullest, then becomes a little city on a hill, a lamp burning throughout the neighborhood to all peoples (see Matt. 5:14–15). While there is no sanctuary lamp in a couple's home, many homes have a Sacred Heart image that spreads its light to every person who enters the house. The couples chronicled in this chapter constructed small arks throughout their lives whereby they carried their children and many others with them to the shores of heaven.

BLESSED LUIGI AND BLESSED MARIA QUATTROCCHI

Luigi and Maria hold the distinction of being the first married couple to be beatified together. This event occurred in 2001, seven years before Saint Thérèse's parents became the second married couple to be beatified. Luigi and Maria hailed from two different worlds. Luigi was born in Catania, Sicily, on January 12, 1880, while Maria was born in Florence on June 24, 1881. At one point, Luigi's childless aunt and uncle adopted him, though he remained in contact with his biological parents. Maria, on the other hand, came from a noble Corsini family.

Divine Providence led Luigi to Rome where he studied law at La Sapienza University. He would later obtain a position with the Inland Revenue Department and other roles with the Italian banks. Maria eventually transferred from her religious school in Rome to a state school. She became a professor of education and a lecturer.

Luigi and Maria's paths would eventually cross in Rome. According to author Joan Carroll Cruz, the couple met "through the friendship of the two families,"[274] reportedly at Maria's parents' house. Perhaps Luigi and Maria's parents had been praying that their children would meet or even secretly arranged the meeting. One of the greatest

---

[274] Cruz, *Saintly Women of Modern Times*, 132.

blessings of any couple is seeing their son or daughter fall in love with the child of one of their friends who also shares the Catholic Faith. It is never too early to begin praying for your child's future spouse. Only in heaven will we know the role that Luigi's and Maria's parents played in setting up one of the Church's holiest marriages.

Luigi and Maria were engaged by March 15, 1905.[275] Luigi was twenty-five and Maria twenty-one. Cruz also noted that the couple "shared intellectual and artistic interests." As mentioned earlier, couples like Luigi and Maria are often drawn to each other because of their mutual interests. One marries someone precisely because he or she shares the same loves: books, politics, philosophy, science, food, entertainment, and most of all, religion. Two highly intelligent people will have deeper discussions. But what about one's greatest love: the Catholic Faith and the Holy Eucharist? Notice Cruz does not mention the shared zeal for their Faith. In fact, Maria was more devout than Luigi. Her son Cesare described his father as, "a good man, just and honest, but not very practicing."[276] But God would use Maria's example to help inspire her husband's piety.

The couple was married on November 25, 1905, in the Basilica of Saint Mary Major in Rome, the largest Marian Church in Rome. They had four children together, three of whom became a diocesan priest, a Benedictine religious superior, and a Trappist monk. Because Maria's health was in jeopardy during her pregnancy with their youngest

---

[275] Cruz, 132.
[276] Burns, *Butler's Lives of the Saints*, 268.

child, Enrichetta, her doctor advised her to have an abortion. Later in life, Enrichetta mentioned that her mother had a five percent chance of survival.[277] Of course this did not matter to Maria—she was going to have her child.

What made this couple so holy was their great love for the spiritual life. The devotions that Maria practiced before meeting Luigi took on a new level after her courtship and marriage. They realized that courtship and marriage was a divine calling to love God more than anything in this life and to help get each other and their children to heaven. As Pope Saint John Paul II stated at their beatification Mass:

> Drawing on the word of God and the witness of the saints, the blessed couple lived *an ordinary life in an extraordinary way.* Among the joys and anxieties of a normal family, they knew how to live an *extraordinarily rich spiritual life.* At the centre of their life was the daily Eucharist as well as devotion to the Virgin Mary, to whom they prayed every evening with the Rosary, and consultation with wise spiritual directors. In this way they could accompany their children in vocational discernment, training them to appreciate everything "from the roof up," as they often, charmingly, liked to say.[278]

---

[277] Cruz, *Saintly Women of Modern Times*, 132.

[278] Pope Saint John Paul II, "Beatification of the Servants of God: Luigi Beltrame Quattrocchi and Maria Corsini, Married Couple," Vatican. va, vatican.va/content/john-paul-ii/en/homilies/2001/documents/hf _jp-ii_hom_20011021_beltrame-quattrocchi.html.

At the center of their marriage was the Eucharist, but also a competent spiritual director helped to guide them to sainthood. According to Cruz, "Both parents were guided by the same spiritual father, a member of the Franciscan Order, and it is not surprising that when they decided to join a Third Order, they chose that of the Franciscans. Maria, for a time, was also under the direction of the Dominican Padre Garrigou Lagrange, the great teacher of mystical and ascetical theology."[279]

Luigi and Maria did not live for themselves or for their children alone. They regularly helped the sick and even welcomed Jewish refugees into their house during World War II. Maria also taught catechesis at a local parish. Stretching themselves so thin across so many apostolates could try their marriage, but their love always overcame any disagreements they had. As Enrichetta once declared, "It is obvious to think that at times they had differences of opinions, but we, their children, were never exposed to these. . . . They solved their problems between themselves, through conversation, so that once they came to an agreement, the atmosphere continued to be serene."[280] Many couples can easily scandalize their children by arguing in front of them, but not this couple. Instead, they allowed Christ's peace and love to permeate their relationship. Luigi and Maria lived their marriage to the fullest. Their children "recalled that their family life was never dull, since there was always time for sports and holidays at the

---

[279] Cruz, *Saintly Women of Modern Times*, 133.
[280] Cruz, 134.

mountains and the sea. And there was also an involvement with a scouting group, organized by their parents for the youths of the poor sections of Rome."[281]

Pope Saint John Paul II further summed up their entire life with these remarkable words, "This couple lived married love and service to life in the light of the Gospel and with great human intensity. With full responsibility they assumed the task of collaborating with God in procreation, dedicating themselves generously to their children, to teach them, guide them and direct them to discovering his plan of love. From this fertile spiritual terrain sprang vocations to the priesthood and the consecrated life, which shows how, with their common roots in the spousal love of the Lord, marriage and virginity may be closely connected and reciprocally enlightening."[282]

In their forty-five years of married life, Luigi and Maria poured themselves out for others, especially their children and the forsaken. It is no wonder that three of their children became Christ's spouses. Those who live their marriage authentically and sacrificially give their children the greatest example.

In 1951, Luigi died from a heart attack at the age of seventy-one. Maria then became a widow for fourteen years before being reunited with her husband. While neither Luigi nor Maria died a martyr's death or became a

---

[281] Cruz, 134.

[282] Pope Saint John Paul II, "Beatification of the Servants of God: Luigi Beltrame Quattrocchi and Maria Corsini, Married Couple," Vatican. va, vatican.va/content/john-paul-ii/en/homilies/2001/documents/hf _jp-ii_hom_20011021_beltrame-quattrocchi.html.

religious, their heroic spousal love spread the gospel to all they met. The Church celebrates their feast day on November 25, the day of their wedding vows.

JOSEPH AND MARIA RATZINGER

When we think about how the parents of a pope met for the first time, we might naturally think they met at Mass or on a pilgrimage to Saint Peter's Basilica. But this devout couple from Bavaria was ahead of their time. Similar to today's online dating sites, Joseph and Maria Ratzinger met by way of a Catholic weekly newspaper advertisement for a marriage partner in the *Altottinger Liebfraubote*. Raised in a peasant family as one of nine children, Joseph Ratzinger eventually became a constable with the rank of an inspector. The advertisement Joseph placed (only recently discovered and reported by the *Catholic News Agency*) declared, "Middle-ranking civil servant, single, Catholic, 43, immaculate past, from the country, is looking for a good Catholic, pure girl who can cook well, tackle all household chores, with a talent for sewing and homemaking with a view to marriage as soon as possible. Fortune desirable but not a precondition."[283] Note Joseph's first requirements for a future spouse: "a good Catholic, pure girl." A virtuous woman is what mattered most to Joseph. His advertisement was spot on: he wanted someone who had the skills to be a good Catholic mother.

---

[283] "Pope's parents met through," Catholic News Agency, September 11, 2006, catholicnewsagency.com/news/7852/popes-parents-met-through-singles-ad.

Thankfully, the thirty-six-year-old Maria responded to the advertisement and four months later they were married on November 9, 1920. Their marriage took place less than seven months after Pope Saint John Paul II was born. Maria did not have a fortune, but she was everything Joseph wanted in a wife. She was experienced with children, as the oldest of eight siblings, and worked at her father's bakery. She was described as being "very warm-hearted and had great inner strength,"[284] a balance to her husband's strict and introverted character. The pope acknowledged his parents as possessing "two very different temperaments and this difference was also exactly what made them complementary."[285]

While we think we know what potential spouse's temperament is best for us, only God truly knows. In our over-sexualized world, how refreshing to know that Joseph Ratzinger sought to live a pure life and marry someone who embraced virtue. Practically speaking, Joseph wanted a lady whose hands were made for cleaning, cooking, and caressing babies rather than manicures and cocktails.

Before their third and youngest child Joseph Aloisius Ratzinger—who would become Pope Benedict XVI—was born on April 16, 1927, Maria Ratzinger gave birth to Maria in 1921 and Georg in 1924. Interestingly, Pope Benedict's parents were ages fifty and forty-three at his birth. Finances kept Pope Benedict's father from getting married sooner, while Maria was needed to help support her family's bakery

---

[284] Seewald, *Benedict XVI*, 125.
[285] Seewald, 125.

business and other endeavors. She was even sent away by her parents to Munich to work as a pastry chef. As Seewald said, "there was no time to get married."[286]

Ironically, many men and women put off marriage for many reasons, such as a career, fear of commitment, or unbridled promiscuity. Others, like Pope Benedict's parents, wanted to get married, but there were too many obstacles in the way. Joseph and Maria would have loved to have had a large family like the ones they came from, but time was not on their side. The important lesson was that Joseph and Maria never gave up on their vocation even when the odds were not in their favor. God clearly fulfilled the desires of Joseph Ratzinger's heart when He gave him a holy woman who not only knew how to cook well but was the daughter of a baker! As always, God shows that He is never outdone in generosity and loves to surprise His children with the greatest gifts, if only we would have a little trust.

Can you imagine Joseph and Maria Ratzinger's shock when they got to heaven and God informed them that their youngest son would become the pope? Their love shows that God can transform the Church and the world more through one holy child, much more so than through any device we invent, any book we write, any speech we give, or any money we leave behind.

Joseph and Maria were blessed with "a happy marriage," according to their middle son, Georg, who became a priest. Amidst the looming rise of Nazism, the couple and their

---

[286] Seewald, 127.

children turned to daily prayer. The future pope loved to play Mass as a child. Thus Joseph and Maria reveal that the best marriages are rooted in the school of the Holy Family, for where there is simplicity, love, poverty of spirit, work, obedience, purity, and humility, there is true happiness. To make one's home a little Holy Trinity and a little Holy Family is to experience paradise now, especially when one's wife knows how to cook!

CHAPTER 9

SAINTLY MATCHMAKERS

"A saint keeps watch over his country and obtains
its salvation. His prayers and virtues are more
powerful than all the armies in the world."[287]

—Saint Peter Julian Eymard

THE FAMOUS SONG "Matchmaker, Matchmaker" orig-
inated in the 1964 musical and later movie, *Fiddler on*
the Roof. The song and plot revolve around a poor Jewish man's three oldest daughters and their desire to find a
spouse. At first, they long to marry someone "interesting,
well off, and important." The town's matchmaker, Yente,
has a perfect match for them, especially since these young
ladies are poor and have few options. But in the end, the
three sisters marry according to the heart and not their
Jewish tradition of arranged marriages.[288]

---

[287] Eymard, *The Real Presence*, 22.
[288] Only a few Jewish communities have arranged marriages today,
such as the Haredi, known for their strict adherence to Jewish Law.
In Haredi Judaism, parents may arrange a marriage for their children.
These parents can also employ a professional matchmaker known as a
shadchan. However, the children may reject their parents' proposal if
either person does not accept the offer.

Many people today would love to have a matchmaker who could lead them to their spouse, provided they are not coerced. Of course, God is the Divine Matchmaker. But we nonetheless have many saintly matchmakers at our disposal. The problem is that we do not call upon their assistance enough. Most people have more earthly friends than heavenly friends. God desires that we become great friends of the saints and invoke their intercession frequently, especially for the most important matters in life: our vocation (choosing a spouse or a religious order), work, conceiving a child. Outside of God Himself, the saints are the greatest matchmakers, for they desire nothing more than to bring two souls together into a marriage that will impact eternity.

The retired Archbishop of Philadelphia Charles Chaput once said, "When young people ask me how to change the world, I tell them to love each other, get married, stay faithful to one another, have lots of children, and raise those children to be men and women of Christian character."[289]

When it comes to matters such as finding a spouse or growing in virtue, the saints want to help us more than we are ready to accept their aid. If we believed that the saints are "more powerful than all the armies in the world," we would always seek their help with the greatest confidence. In fact, many saints were working miracles long before they were canonized. While many of us would have loved to

[289] "Archbishop Chaput: 'the future belongs to people with children, not with things,'" Lifesite News, August 1, 2017, www.lifesitenews.com/news/archbishop-chaput-the-future-belongs-to-people-with-children-not-with-thing/.

have befriended Saint Josemaría Escrivá or Saint Padre Pio while they lived on earth, the truth is that they can assist us even more from heaven. Truly, a just man's intercessory prayer, whether he prays from earth or heaven, "availeth much" (Jas. 5:16). A just man's prayers are powerful and effective. Since the saints were God's best friends, He can refuse them nothing if it be in accordance with His will.

TOMÁS AND PAQUITA ALVIRA

On February 19, 2009, Spanish couple Tomás and Paquita Alvira's cause of canonization was opened. Unlike many who meet their spouse and shortly thereafter marry within a few years, this couple's courtship, interrupted by the Spanish Civil War, lasted over thirteen years. In the end, their courtship stood the test of time, just like their marriage. Many people "fall in love" at first sight like Tomás and Paquita, but not every attraction ends up on the altar. If it is true love rooted in God and not infatuation, it will endure—but not without difficulty. The greatest love is always proved in the crucible of suffering and waiting.

Long before they bore nine children, there was the unforgettable meeting on January 23, 1926, on a school field trip from Zaragoza to Barcelona. Tomás's father, also named Tomás, was Paquita's principal. Young Tomás, twenty-years old at the time and a student at the University of Zaragoza, was asked to come along. While on the train, he locked eyes with fourteen-year-old Paquita Dominguez on several occasions. The 185-mile, seven-hour train trip led to Tomás and Paquita's meeting. According to author

Olga Emily Marlin, "Tomás's eyes met Paquita's several times; she noticed that he was looking at her, and was pleased. That was the spark that set off a blaze that would never go out."[290] Marlin goes on to say, "When he (Tomás) first saw her, Paquita was surely not wearing something new, that could be ruined by cinders of the train: but she did have an attractive feminine grace. Her wavy chestnut hair fell softly around her face, and her serene brown eyes shone with admiration. For Tomás it was love at first sight, and from that moment he never looked at anyone else."[291]

Tomás would lose his father from tuberculosis a year later. The patriach's death had a ripple effect on the family. They moved to the city where Tomás became the head of the household. He was also required to do military service. But after his brief stint in the military, Tomás embarked on a teaching career just like his father. Because Paquita was incredibly young when they first met, it would be years before they were married. Despite the tumult of the Spanish Civil War raging for three years (1936–1939), "Tomás and Paquita kept their love alive through letters and the occasional visit that Tomás could make to Zaragoza."[292] In the midst of this separation, there was resignation to God's will. Or in the words of Tomás, "But we didn't ask for this; it's something that can't be helped. We have to bear it."[293] In order to get married sooner and so provide for his future spouse, Tomás intensified his studies. He told Paquita, also

---

[290] Marlin, *Our Lives in His Hands*, 1.
[291] Marlin, 1.
[292] Marlin, 21.
[293] Marlin, 21.

studying to be a teacher, "at every moment my thoughts go to you—and that gives me the strength to study all the harder, because of you and for you. Will God will to help me? Pray a lot, and very hard, that he will. No matter what, I will always love you with all my heart. Your Tomás."[294]

The couple wondered at times if their courtship would endure because of the Civil War. Tomás's life was threatened on several occasions. On one occasion, he rescued his twenty-two-year-old sister, who was a novice for the Sisters of Charity in Madrid. Priests and consecrated souls were often targeted by the leftist coalition.[295]

During the war, God sent Tomás a spiritual guide to help him in his sufferings and separation from Paquita. His name was Saint Josemaría Escrivá. Upon meeting the saint through a mutual friend, Tomás immediately opened his heart to him. Tomás never wanted to leave his spiritual father, so much so that he and a few others once fled temporarily with Saint Josemaría to France on a perilous journey.

As Opus Dei[296] grew, Tomás began to wonder if God was calling him to lead a celibate life like the first followers. Even though Tomás was engaged at the time, Saint Josemaría told him, "You should get married and wait; there

---

[294] Marlin, 22.

[295] The Spanish Civil War, also known as the "Red Terror," resulted in the deaths of 4,000 priests, over 2,000 monks, and nearly 300 nuns. On March 11, 2001, Pope Saint John Paul II beatified 233 martyrs from the Spanish Civil War.

[296] Opus Dei, meaning the "work of God" was founded in 1928 by Saint Josemaría Escrivá to remind people of the universal call to holiness. Its membership includes priests, lay celibates, married, and single people.

will be something else for you."[297] Paquita felt indebted to Saint Josemaría for this selfless counsel, since Tomás could have given himself more fully to Opus Dei's mission. Later, Opus Dei would welcome lay members. Saint Josemaría is not a "matchmaker" in the strictest sense like the saint featured in the next story, who literally helped bring two souls together for marriage. However, Saint Josemaría steered Tomás to the vocation God wanted for him.[298] On his deathbed, Tomás declared to his youngest son, also named Tomás, "My son, from the time I first met him I put my life in his hands."[299]

Patience would again be the story of Tomás and Paquita's courtship as they could not marry due to the war and Tomás's obligation to take care of his widowed mother and sister. But once the war ended, Tomás and Paquita could finally get married. Saint Josemaría had planned to preside at their wedding, but a delay from a retreat prevented him. On June 16, 1939, Tomás and Paquita exchanged vows at the Church of Saint Giles in Zaragoza. Because of the war and the couple's poverty, only a small group of family and friends attended. Although both Tomás and Paquita's earthly fathers were not there in person to witness that blessed day, perhaps God gave them front row seats from the choir loft of heaven. Marlin provides further details of the wedding: "Paquita wore an elegant suit, instead of

---

[297] Marlin, *Our Lives in His Hands*, 40.
[298] One major mistake of spiritual directors and vocation directors is to "recruit" young men and women for the priesthood or religious life rather than guide them to the vocation that God wants for their lives.
[299] Marlin, *Our Lives in His Hands*, 37.

a wedding gown, and the rings were of silver, not gold. The reception meal was a splendid breakfast."[300] For their honeymoon, the couple went to San Sebastian and then the Cantabrian Coast.

The honeymoon period ended quickly only a few weeks after their wedding, when Tomás told Paquita that he would be going on a retreat with his spiritual father. At first, Paquita was taken aback. But with time, she came to understand "all that Father meant to him."[301] Saint Josemaría became not only the spiritual father to Tomás and Paquita but also to their children. Saint Josemaría baptized their first child José María Tomás, certainly after the future saint and his own father. Sadly, this child died unexpectedly at the age of five from illness, drawing this couple even more to heaven. In the words of Tomás, "The eldest was José María. He was very handsome, and very charming; but he very soon departed to heaven . . . to prepare the way for all the rest of us."[302] Tomás and Paquita saw God's goodness even in the midst of the most horrendous suffering. They had a supernatural outlook and maintained their serenity no matter the crosses accorded to their children. But what stood out was the freedom they gave to their children. They never tried to conform their children into their own image, but into Christ's. Miraculously, all eight children were involved in Opus Dei.

When Tomás died in 1992, Paquita declared, "I will be going soon, because without him I am only half of

---

[300] Marlin, 59.
[301] Marlin, 60.
[302] Marlin, 70.

myself."[303] Two years later, Paquita was reunited once again with her husband and their firstborn son. Unlike many couples who experience love at first sight, but that love eventually fades, Tomás and Paquita's love deepened over time. In the words of their son Rafael Alvira, "My parents persevered in their eagerness to love one another right to the end of their lives. A friend of one of my sisters told her that she was envious of my parents, because she would see them walking in the street and could tell that they still loved each other as when they were dating. As the years went by, my parents had the same eagerness that they had the day they got married, and their love was always increasing."[304]

Couples like the Alviras, whose love is rooted in the cross of Christ, will always find an inexhaustible fount of grace to keep the embers of their love burning. The real secret to their love was Saint John's words, "Let us therefore love God, because God first hath loved us" (1 Jn. 4:19). Every morning Tomás and Paquita engaged in thirty minutes of mental prayer. In addition, Tomás attended daily Mass. The contemplative life spilled over to every facet of their daily life, most notably their love for each other and their love for their children. Their daughter Pilar once commented, "I felt an incomparable joy in realizing how much I was loved. Their affection ran so

---

[303] Marlin, 197.

[304] "His Parents are on the path to sainthood. He says these are the secrets of their family," Aleteia, October 24, 2019, aleteia.org/2019/10/24 /his-parents-are-on-path-to-sainthood-he-says-these-are-the-secr ets-of-their-family-life/#.

deep, it was so unselfish, the gratitude and joy on their faces when I arrived in the evening were such that I often asked myself what the love of God must be like in heaven, when seeing myself loved like this was bringing me so much happiness."[305] The spiritual masters would often use a ladder to describe the path toward heaven. In a similar way, a holy marriage becomes like a holy ladder where God's love descends down from the parents and the parents help bring their children up to God.

DR. GERMAIN AND ORTRUD BIANCHI[306]

My name is Ortrud Bianchi and I was born in 1945 in Ronsperg, Czech Republic, the youngest of six children. Several months after my birth, we settled in a small town in Germany. My parents, Sieplinde and Erhard Schumann divorced when I was five years old. There was no religious atmosphere in our home, but I did receive religious instruction in school as well as the sacraments of the Catholic Church. On rare occasions, my brother and I attended church. Watching my mother's difficult life as a divorcée convinced me that I would remain single.

When I was a teenager, my maternal grandmother, who lived in Austria, died unexpectedly. My mother traveled to the funeral and decided to remain in Austria. She realized that life can end abruptly, and, by the grace of God,

---

[305] Marlin, *Our Lives in His Hands*, 140.

[306] The following story was originally published in Allen, *Pray, Hope, and Don't Worry: True Stories of Padre Pio Book 1*, Chap. 44. Used with permission.

she began to practice her Catholic Faith with great fervor, making up for lost time.

As a result of my mother's move to Austria, I joined my oldest sister and her husband in Landshut, Germany, and finished my schooling there. I looked forward to school vacations so that I could be with my mother in Austria. However, I soon noticed that my mother was on a major mission to convert us children. The more she tried to convert us, the more our opposition grew. I finally made my mother promise not to mention religion to me anymore, otherwise I would discontinue my visits to her. My mother complied. The next time I saw her, she kept silent about her faith in God. When it was time to say goodbye, she handed me a small pamphlet to take home with me. On the cover of it was a picture of Jesus. That was a dead give-away to me that it was a religious pamphlet, therefore boring and a waste of time to read. But I took it anyway, in order to avoid an argument.

Months passed and Easter vacation was about to begin. The pamphlet! Suddenly I remembered. Without fail, my mother's first question would be to ask me how I liked it. The easiest solution would be to read just one small page and then I would be off the hook.

I was home alone and opened the pamphlet randomly. It was from the diary of the Polish nun, Sister (now Saint) Faustina Kowalska. My eyes fell on the text where Jesus explained to Sister Faustina that His mercy was greater than any human or angelic mind could ever fathom. Jesus invited every soul, no matter how sinful, to draw close to His merciful heart. The words hit me like lightning.

Jesus loves me! Why be indifferent to the One who loves me more than I can ever imagine? Overwhelmed by deep emotions of contrition, I felt a force that brought me to my knees. I began to cry and I repeated over and over, "Jesus, from now on I want to be your friend."

The next morning, Sunday, I got up and got ready for church while a puzzled and disbelieving sister and brother-in-law looked on. I made my way to church for confession and Mass. I never missed another Sunday Mass after that, and I began to pray for all of the members of my family.

By July, 1964, I lived with my mother in Austria. Two years later, my youngest brother and his fiancée were meeting the rest of the family in Rome for their wedding. They mailed the necessary documents for the wedding to Rome and made sure that they were certified, insured, and registered. The documents for their wedding disappeared and were never found. Because of that, they were not able to get married.

While everyone was devastated that there would be no wedding, my mother cheerfully announced that she had "Plan B." A friend had recently informed her of a holy monk, Padre Pio, who had the stigmata and lived in San Giovanni Rotondo. What a perfect opportunity it would be to visit him, since everyone was already in Rome. As we traveled to Padre Pio's monastery, I became more and more excited at the thought of seeing a saint.

Our first experience was to be present for the opening of the church doors at 4:50 a.m. for Padre Pio's 5:00 a.m. Mass. People started to push and shove, causing my brother-in-law to lose his shoe. Another person's glasses flew off. Inside the church, people were racing down the middle aisle and jumping over the pews. It was like a sports event.

Then Padre Pio entered the sanctuary. He looked old, weak, and even sickly. I could tell that he was suffering and I felt sorry for him. I thought it would be better for him to have some bed rest rather than to be surrounded by people who seemed more devoted to him than to Jesus and Mary. "Why do these people bother Padre Pio, trying to talk to him and touch him?" I said to myself. "I think they are on the wrong track. They are misled. Don't they know that we have Jesus in the Blessed Sacrament? We don't have to run after a person!"

I watched Padre Pio celebrate Mass and nothing extraordinary happened. Somehow I expected holiness to be radiating from him that would at least cause me to have some goose-bumps. Nothing happened inside of me. My final resolve was that I had seen Padre Pio once and that was good enough. There was no need to ever return to San Giovanni Rotondo again.

Two years later, my mother and a young man who was a fellow member of the Legion of Mary and I made a pilgrimage to the shrine of Our Lady of Loreto in Italy. We had a wonderful time there. My mother suggested that we drive to San Giovanni Rotondo to see Padre Pio. It was a distance of at least 230 miles and there were no highways at that time to get there, only small roads. I told my mother that our car was too old and unreliable to make the trip. Besides, she had already seen Padre Pio. However, all my reasoning with my mother was to no avail. She told me that if I would not take her, she would walk the distance by herself. I told my mother that I would take her, but only because I was a good daughter.

It wasn't too long before our 1949 Volkswagen broke down. Our friend from the Legion of Mary had to hitch-hike back to the previous town, and, since he did not speak Italian, he had to try to explain in sign language the car parts he needed to purchase in order to fix our car. My mother and I sat in a ditch as we prayed the Rosary and waited for him to return.

It took several hours to get the car running again. About 9:00 p.m. the car broke a second time. There was no mechanic shop anywhere near, and by now everything was closed. We grabbed our few belongings, locked the car, and hitchhiked through the night to San Giovanni Rotondo. When we reached the monastery at 5:00 a.m., my mother was overjoyed and made a solemn proclamation, "Isn't God good! We have arrived on time for Holy Mass." After Mass, we met a German lady on the plaza in front of the church. She knew how to get tickets to go to confession to Padre Pio and how to get tickets to enter the sacristy where Padre Pio passed after the morning confessions.

My mother obtained tickets, and the next morning along with about fifteen other women we were ushered into the old sacristy. It was no big deal for me. This time around I knew better than to expect anything. I knew that Padre Pio was just a human being. Yes, he might be a saint, but I felt it was selfish to bother him the way the people did. "I will just play the game along with my mother," I said to myself.

The door opened and there stood Padre Pio. We all knelt down for his blessing as he passed in front of each person. He stopped in front of my mother, looked at her, and blessed her. I was next. He then placed his hand on my head. My whole body felt that touch. It felt like electricity going through my body and at the same time my soul was touched. I can't explain what happened, but I knew that something had taken place. I knew that a strong bond, a deep spiritual relationship between Padre Pio and myself had been established. He had become my spiritual father and I had become his adopted spiritual daughter. I ran outside the church and started to cry.

Back in Austria, I could not stop talking about Padre Pio. My two sisters, brother, brother-in-law, mother, and I decided, only three weeks after my return from San Giovanni Rotondo, to take a trip together to see Padre Pio. Being back in San Giovanni Rotondo felt like being in Heaven, and the days we spent there were pure happiness. We stayed for several weeks. I finally realized that the people who came to the monastery to see Padre Pio were not selfish like I had first thought. They were there for the same reason that I was there. Without even saying anything, Padre Pio was taking us closer to Jesus. Just looking at Padre Pio made you want to love Jesus more. He was like a magnet, drawing people closer and closer to God.

The morning of August 25, 1966, was our planned departure and we packed all our luggage in the trunk for our return trip back to Austria. At that moment, I decided to stay in San Giovanni Rotondo and I removed my bag from the car. As a religious education teacher, I still had three weeks of vacation left and I wanted to stay as long as possible. My family tried to reason with me and said to me, "You don't know the Italian language. You don't have money for a hotel. You don't have money for the train ticket back to Austria. You do not even have enough money for food!" "I am twenty-one years old and I can make my own decisions," I replied. I loved Padre Pio (like all those crazy Italian women), and all I cared about was to be near him.

After I said goodbye to my family, I went back to the church to pray. When I was near Padre Pio, all of my earthly desires seemed to disappear. Being close to him was like being on a retreat. During the afternoon, I asked about lodging but could not find anything in my price range. I asked the German lady who had befriended me if she knew of a place I could stay overnight, but she did not know of anything.

After the evening Benediction service, everyone had to leave as the church doors were locked. Slowly, with my bag over my shoulder, I made my way across the plaza. My happy feeling made way for a pressing question, "What now? Where do I sleep?" I did not have money for a hotel and sleeping out in the open air under the stars made me nervous. Not only were there snakes in the area but also stray dogs.

I uttered a short prayer to Padre Pio, "Dear Padre Pio, I have never prayed to you for myself, but now I need your help. Please help me to find a place to sleep tonight." As I finished my cry for help, I noticed that a young man, who was sitting on a bench under a tree, got up and started walking toward me. We talked for a few minutes, and then

I informed him that I had to be on my way for I had to find a place to stay for the night. He asked me to wait on the bench and he would be back soon. With no place to go, the bench seemed very inviting.

Fifteen minutes passed and then he returned. "Come, follow me," he said. "I found a place for you to stay." We headed down a hill to the first house across from the monastery. He led me into the house, down the stairs, and opened the door to a room furnished with three beds. Pointing to the bed on the right he said, "This one is yours. It is fifty cents a night." I thanked him, and he left. Shortly after there was a knock at the door. To my surprise, it was the young man again. He handed me two paper bags, smiled, and said, "This is for you. Good night." Inside the bags were two delicious sandwiches, an apple, and a pear. My mind was racing. How did he know that I had not eaten a meal that day?

The next morning an Italian lady who stayed at the same residence invited me to a little room and served me a big dish of pasta with bread and wine. "Mangia, mangia," (eat, eat) she said, but I really did not need any encouragement, and I ate all the food.

That day I ran into the young man again. I learned that he was an American studying medicine in Rome. He had arrived in Rome in August, but his school was closed until September. He felt inspired to spend his free time in San Giovanni Rotondo near Padre Pio.

There was no lack of German-speaking pilgrims at the monastery, and one day I met a woman named Adelinde from Austria. She urged me to pray for her intention. She confided to me that she was anxious about traveling alone and that she would like Padre Pio to send her a traveling companion for her return trip back to Austria.

I told her that her worries were over. Padre Pio had answered her prayers, and she was looking at her traveling companion. The idea popped into my mind that it would be great to have a man in the car, in case we had a flat tire. Adelinde agreed, and the American was offered a free ride to Rome, which he accepted. Leaving San Giovanni Rotondo the following week was extremely painful to me. The thought of returning soon was the only thing that made it bearable. The three of us traveled to Rome together, and, once in Rome, Adelinde had some business to take care of and excused herself for a half hour.

While waiting in the car for Adelinde to return, I suggested to the American that we pray the Rosary together. I led the first part of the Hail Mary in German and he answered in English. Adelinde came back, and we continued our journey. On the way to the hotel to drop off the American, I felt a hand on my right shoulder. It was the American. The strange thing was that it did not feel like a human hand. I experienced the exact same powerful feeling in my body as when Padre Pio put his hand on my head. The feeling lasted as long as the young man's hand was on my shoulder. Before leaving the car, he handed me a piece of paper with his name and address and asked for mine. The card he handed me said, "Germain Bianchi, Yonkers, New York."

Several days after I returned to my home in Austria, the doorbell rang, and, when I opened the door, there stood the American. I wanted to introduce him to my mother, but I could not remember his name. He came to visit me again, just three weeks later. Traveling such a long distance to see me alarmed me, so I had a talk with him.

I began by saying, "I am not interested in any close relationships. I am very happy being single and I want to remain single. I don't want to divide my love for Jesus. I like to go to church whenever I please and pray. I love being a religious education teacher. I would never want to take the chance of getting married. These days people make promises and later it is a different story."

Germain listened, and, after a pause, he responded to each point I had made. He said to me, "You are very happy to be single, but it is also possible to be happy as a married person. You should never divide your love for Jesus. Neither would I. Rather we would help each other to love Jesus more and more. And I would never be unfaithful to you. You have my word."

"Ortrud, stick to your principles," I said to myself. "Don't give in. Don't get weak!" But I could feel my heart softening just a bit. "Why are we discussing marriage?" I said to Germain. "I don't even know you and you don't know me." "I know you well enough," Germain said, "that I would like to ask you to marry me. When we were sitting in the car and you asked me to pray the Rosary with you, you were the first girl that ever asked me to pray the Rosary. I knew then that I wanted you to be my wife."

The next day Germain took a train to San Giovanni Rotondo. In confession, he told Padre Pio that he met a girl that he wanted to marry but that she was not sure about him. Padre Pio, a man of few words, advised him, "Marry her and prepare well for your marriage." Germain heard what he wanted to hear, but I still needed my own sign.

At Christmas time, I went to San Giovanni Rotondo, and Germain was there with me. I wanted to ask Padre Pio about marrying Germain. One day I happened to have an excellent position in the front row of a crowded sacristy. There were many other women there as well. Padre Pio would be passing within two feet of me, and at that time I planned on speaking to him about Germain.

Brother Joseph Pius, one of the Capuchins who lived at the monastery, approached me and motioned for me to follow him. I told him that I was in an excellent spot to talk to Padre Pio, but he insisted that I go with him. I was not thrilled to give up my good place in the front row, but I followed Brother Joseph Pius. He led me through the big church, unlocked the door to the monastery, and gave me orders to wait there in the middle of a long hallway. A few minutes later he reappeared with Germain, whom he had found in the upstairs hallway waiting with the men for Padre Pio to pass by. He told Germain to stand next to me, and then he left without any explanation.

Before we could figure out who had arranged this interesting happening, the door at the end of the hallway opened, and Padre Pio, aided by two friars, entered. Knowing that Padre Pio could see into the souls of people, my first reaction was to look down toward the floor and avoid eye contact. Instead, I looked straight into his beautiful brown eyes the entire time he was walking slowly towards us. When he reached us, he stopped. He put his hand on

Germain's head, then on my head, and with one blessing, he blessed us both together. No words were spoken,
no angel appeared, but I received my sign. I knew at that
moment that Germain and I were meant to be together
and to marry.

I continued to visit Padre Pio every time I had a vacation. On August 15, 1967, Germain and I became officially
engaged. Germain had an engagement ring made for me
from a gold miraculous medal surrounded by tiny pearls.
Padre Pio kept the ring in his room for many days and
blessed it in time for our engagement. Our wedding was
on the Feast of the Assumption, August 15, 1968. Padre
Pio no longer performed weddings in his later years due to
his poor health, but he was taken in his wheelchair to meet
us before the wedding ceremony began. Germain thanked
him for everything. Padre Pio blessed our wedding rings
and gave us his blessing. Then he tapped me three times
on my head. I felt as though he had opened a valve inside
of me for I felt a happiness that was indescribable. By the
end of the day I said, "God has to take this feeling away for
I feel my heart is ready to burst with joy."

Our wedding took place in the church of Our Lady of
Grace where Padre Pio had received the stigmata, celebrated Mass for most of his life, and heard daily confessions. Father Ermelindo celebrated the wedding Mass. In
the afternoon, Brother Joseph Pius and Father Ermelindo
surprised us at the wedding reception with their presence.
Brother Joseph Pius made this announcement to us, "Germain and Ortrud, I hope you will enjoy this wedding gift
from Padre Pio. Because he is often sick, he no longer signs

pictures or cards. Instead, we sign them for him. I asked him what I should write on the back of this picture of Our Lady of Grace and Padre Pio answered me, "Give me the picture and let me sign it myself." Padre Pio wrote, "Maria vi tenga stretta nel sua amore." (May the Virgin Mary hold you tightly in her love.) For our honeymoon we did not go to a beach resort or vacation spot. We stayed in San Giovanni Rotondo for several weeks, the best place on earth.

One month after our wedding, we heard the very sad news that Padre Pio had died. We went to San Giovanni Rotondo to attend the funeral. As we stood in line to pass by Padre Pio's coffin and pay our last respects, an Italian woman kept tapping me on the shoulder, advising me to ask Padre Pio for something when I paused at his casket. I did what she suggested. As I stood at his coffin, I prayed, "Padre Pio, please bless our marriage with a child." Nine months later, our first son was born. It is said that our prayers are often answered in a more abundant way than what we ask. We were blessed with eight beautiful children, the last being twins. The twins were born on the feast of Our Lady of Grace, the patroness of San Giovanni Rotondo. Padre Pio didn't just bring us together, he has taken care of us ever since. His fatherly care and love has been with us for almost forty years of married life.

CHAPTER 10

THE GOOD WINE
FOR LAST

"Every man at first setteth forth good wine, and
when men have well drunk, then that which is worse.
But thou hast kept the good wine until now."

—John 2:10

AT THE WEDDING feast of Cana, Our Lord gave the guests the greatest wine in the history of the world, a wine that would three years later be eclipsed on the cross by His very blood. Marriage is the last stage of courtship. It is the pinnacle of human love, a reflection of Christ's love for His Church. Yet it is also just the beginning. In a sense, marriage on earth becomes almost like the first stage of courtship in heaven. Although we will not be married to our earthly spouse in heaven, we will be married to God, our heavenly Spouse. And through this marriage, we will grow in deeper union with Him, falling more in love with the three persons of the Most Blessed Trinity forever. Heaven is the perpetual honeymoon where we partake of God

Himself, should we persevere and should He have mercy on our souls.

God always saves the best for last. No good father gives his children everything all at once. If he did, his children would not appreciate everything that came before it. In a similar way, God the Father has given us this great sacrament of marriage so that we might experience glimpses of eternity, such as meeting your spouse for the first time, seeing your spouse walk down the aisle, seeing your bride unveiled on your wedding night, and peering into your child's eyes. And the thought that either you or your spouse will be waiting for each other on the other side fills you with longing and hope for the eternal reunion with God.

The following courtship stories offer one last glimpse of how love can be found through a friend or while making a pilgrimage. Interestingly, both couples are Italian, and so wine would have been a part of their courtship and marriage. When you think the wine has run dry, when adversity sets in, and you have given up all hope of meeting your spouse or you want to give up, Our Lord comes to serve you "the good wine." Yes, God loves to spoil His children when they least expect it, as seen throughout this book, often in the most ordinary of ways.

VENERABLE VITTORIO AND ROSALIA TRANCANELLI

William Shakespeare's tragedy *Romeo and Juliet* is the most famous love story ever written. It chronicles the lives of two Italian lovers whose families despise one another.

Despite the obstacles, Romeo and Juliet get married, though sadly they end up dying from suicide. When Venerable Vittorio and Rosalia Trancanelli[307] were married on October 18, 1970, in the Abbey of San Salvatore and San Lorenzo near Florence, they faced great opposition. No, the families did not hate one another, but when Vittorio was set upon marrying Rosalia, Vittorio's father tried to prevent their marriage.

Four years older than Rosalia Sabatini, Vittorio met her for the first time in Perugia, where Vittorio hailed from. Vittorio was studying at one of the colleges and lived in the same dormitory with a man named Giovanni Sabatini. Vittorio and Giovanni became close friends. Now and then, Giovanni's little sister Rosalia would visit her brother. And so, Vittorio became quickly acquainted with his friend's beautiful younger sister from Tuscany. For Vittorio, it was love at first sight, but not for Rosalia. Vittorio's shy nature prevented him from having the courage to tell Rosalia his true feelings for some time. According to Dr. Enrico Solinas, Vittorio didn't talk much. But, when he spoke, his words were important and full of divine wisdom. Vittorio's reticence was one reason their courtship lasted four years. Vittorio was also occupied with his studies; he would later become an emergency room medical surgeon.

Over time, Rosalia fell more in love with Vittorio as her feelings changed. According to Solinas, "The thing that

---

[307] For the following information, I am indebted to Dr. Enrico Solinas and his translator, Mattia Iannello, in an interview given on January 18, 2022. Dr. Enrico Solinas became the postulator for the cause of Venerable Vittorio in 2012.

convinced her that Vittorio was the man of her life was that she always felt peace when with Vittorio. She never felt this before."[308] Rosalia was also inspired by Vittorio's strong yet hidden relationship with the Lord. Although devout, Vittorio didn't broadcast his piety. Like her, Vittorio wanted to serve God and others. This was another reason Rosalia realized that Vittorio was the one for her. He had a generous and loving heart, a heart of service. At one point, Vittorio wanted to be a missionary in Africa, but God had other plans—plans to serve in his hometown and to marry the love of his life.

Besides her beauty, Vittorio was endeared to Rosalia's simplistic and trustworthy nature. He had always prayed and searched for that type of lady. Rosalia hailed from a simple and normal environment in the small mountain town of Abbadia San Salvatore, unlike Vittorio, who grew up very wealthy. For Vittorio, wealth and prestige did not matter, but for Vittorio's father—it was everything. Because Rosalia was from a low social class, Vittorio's father opposed his son's courtship from the beginning. He wanted his son to marry a woman of high social class, especially in light of his son's prestigious medical career. Vittorio's father was influenced by human respect because he cared more about what people thought about his family than how God or his son felt. Vittorio's father was thinking with a purely secular mindset, which strained his relationship with his son.

His father's view was the opposite of what Vittorio was looking for. Rosalia's modest upbringing endeared her to

---

[308] Dr. Enrico Solinas, interview by author, January 18, 2022.

Vittorio. One's home environment and how one is raised can determine one's growth in virtue, whether one is vain or humble. In Vittorio's case, he wanted someone who cared less about worldly matters and more about heavenly matters. Vittorio and Rosalia's love grew out of friendship, the first stage of courtship. Vittorio and Rosalia would often visit when Rosalia came to see her brother at the university. Sometimes Vittorio also visited Giovanni's house in Tuscany.

Over the course of their courtship, Vittorio wrote over eighty letters to Rosalia—most of which remain unpublished. Vittorio's shy nature, especially in sentimental relationships, can be seen in his letters. He struggled to share his feelings with Rosalia but nevertheless persevered. In May 1967, Vittorio overcame his shyness with boldness and proposed to Rosalia, who happily accepted. No information is provided as to where this sacred moment occurred.

On May 31, 1967, Vittorio wrote the following letter (a small portion is presented here) to his fiancée, Rosalia:

> . . . I think that this gift we were given by the Lord should not be locked up between us, but the love that unites us should spread from us to all the others, to all the people who surround us and to those we don't even know, only then will we really love each other and really be happy in the Lord. We should never close ourselves off because then we would dry up and so would our love. There are so many people who don't even know what happiness is, we should be always ready to bring them some of it, not as we

were giving alms, but as something genuine we were
given and we give to others. With this serenity in our
soul and holding our hands we will always have to
walk through the routes of the world . . .[309]

From the onset of their courtship, Vittorio believed that
God had a special plan for Rosalia and himself. He prayed
that it would end in marriage. Based on his letter, he saw
his future marriage as missionary focused (a calling within
a calling). Indeed, every courtship and marriage ought
to point to Christ and His Church, as Saint Paul wrote,
"For this cause shall a man leave his father and mother,
and shall cleave to his wife, and they shall be two in one
flesh. This is a great sacrament; but I speak in Christ and in
the church. Nevertheless let every one of you in particular
love his wife as himself: and let the wife fear her husband"
(Eph. 5:31–33). The latter verse, one of the most common
readings at weddings, sums up Vittorio and Rosalia's love.

The following month, on June 12, 1967, Vittorio wrote
again to Rosalia:

Rosalia,

You are asking for how much time I have loved
you. Since when I started thinking. Since I am who
I am. That I started looking for you since . . . since
forever. I had an image of a woman in my mind, and
I was looking for that woman. Now I know that the
woman is you. In the past sometimes I have made
some misjudgments. And I committed mistakes

---

[309] Solinas, *Servo di Dio Vittorio Trancanelli*, 19–20.

> about the name I gave to this woman. I was a soul
> in pain. You are the woman of my life. And I want to
> keep knowing you deeply every day.[310]

Vittorio's letter hearkens back to Venerable Fulton Sheen's words, "Everyone carries within his heart a blueprint of his ideal love."[311] It must be noted that Vittorio did discern the call to the priesthood or was at least open to it, but he was certain that God wanted him to be a husband and father. He knew that she was the woman he had prayed and longed for when he met Rosalia for the first time. And he would never let her go unless God wanted him to release her. Most people discerning marriage have an ideal in their hearts of what they dream for in their future spouse. Perhaps it is an image like Vittorio had, consisting of certain physical characteristics, virtues, and temperaments. And that blueprint was stamped in our hearts by God.

For God, this ideal love, before the foundation of the world, was the Blessed Mother.[312] Unlike the Immaculate Virgin Mary, our ideal will never be perfect. As Sheen further stated, "The best of human loves, no matter how devoted they be, must end—and there is nothing perfect that ends."[313] Still, these desires, this image that God put in Vittorio's heart, is something every person discerning

---

[310] This letter has yet to be published per Rosalia. After her death, these letters will be published. This letter came by way of my interview with Dr. Enrico Solinas.
[311] Sheen, *The World's First Love*, 13.
[312] Sheen, 13.
[313] Sheen, 13.

marriage should listen to with the ears of his heart. At the same time, one must temper his expectations.[314] As is often said, perfect is the enemy of the good. Reality is often truer than the ideal.

In another letter written on January 20, 1969, just nine months before his wedding, Vittorio wrote to Rosalia:

> Trying to love The One up there as we are doing more or less well, as we are able to, doesn't mean becoming little nuns or monks and I like you the way you are, all of you with what you are, do or think. It is not the first time I tell you that, is it? After all, The One up there is our only help, our hope, and talking to Him every now and then makes us feel good inside not only individually, but the two of us together. By now between us there's something like a channel so that when one of us does or thinks something, it's like the other one does or thinks it too.[315]

Again, we see Vittorio's deepening love for his future bride. As Vittorio moved through the stages of courtship, he wanted to love her as God loved her—completely and unconditionally. Often, the more you get to know someone, the more glaring that person's sins and weaknesses become. But the opposite seemed the case for Vittorio: the more he saw Rosalia's flaws, the more he loved her. He came to accept and even cherish Rosalia. "I like you the way you are," he wrote to her, "all of you with what you

---

[314] See paragraph "Be Realistic" in *For Those Discerning Marriage* in the back of this book.
[315] Solinas, *Servo di Dio Vittorio Trancanelli*, 21.

are, do or think."[316] Even after their engagement, Vittorio's father tried to break up the relationship by provoking Rosalia. Remarkably, Rosalia never hated her future father-in-law for his indifference and opposition to her.

The couple married on October 18, 1970, in the town of Abbadia San Salvatore, near Tuscany, in a beautiful Catholic Church. In this land dotted with vineyards, there was no chance the wine would run out at this wedding. Since there are no coincidences in life, Vittorio was married on the feast of Saint Luke the Evangelist, the patron of physicians. In fact, many saints chose certain wedding dates based on their favorite feast days.

For their honeymoon, the couple went to Genoa in Northern Italy, a city dubbed by several prominent writers and composers as one of the most beautiful places on earth. But the threats to Vittorio and Rosalia's courtship did not end after their marriage and honeymoon. Because Vittorio's father wanted the newlyweds to remain close to him, they lived with Vittorio's parents. This arrangement wasn't all bad, as it allowed the young couple to save money. But it soon became clear that it would not work. Vittorio and Rosalia had to find a different living situation to protect their marriage.

Although Vittorio's father never tried to end his son's marriage, he still tried to exhort his authority over his son. As much as it pained the couple, Vittorio and Rosalia had to slowly distance themselves from Vittorio's family. The cross of having to constantly choose sides weighed heavy

---

[316] Dr. Enrico Solinas, interview by author, January 18, 2022.

on Vittorio. He wanted to respect his family but be true to his wife. The decision, though difficult, was already made when he courted Rosalia. He would choose her and fight for his marriage. She had won his heart and he promised to God that he would stay with her until death.[317] This of course made Rosalia happy. After landing a more stable position at the hospital in Perugia, the couple moved there.

Besides Rosalia, Vittorio had another love: his patients. He is remembered for being one of the most skilled emergency room surgeons in Perugia, often referred to as "The Saint of the Operating Room." Sometimes he worked for thirty-six hours straight. The long hours did not bother Rosalia as much as you would expect, or at least not for the reasons you might think. She respected his desire to help his patients, she merely worried about him when she did not hear from him. She also worried for his health when he would forget to eat. So she started to walk to the hospital and bring him his lunch.

Vittorio's strong prayer life guided his career as a surgeon. For instance, his colleagues often noticed him sitting

---

[317] In the stages of courtship, it is important that one's family members meet and approve of one's future spouse. At the same time, a father or mother's reasons for opposing the courtship must be grounded in truth and virtue. Parents should not oppose a courtship if one spouse does not come from money or for other secular reasons. Still the question must be asked: can this young man provide for my daughter? A holy courtship should never divide the family but unite it. In some cases, a person will choose a godly spouse even against the parents' wishes, provided that person is truly a holy man or holy woman and will lead them to heaven. Saint John of the Cross's own father was renounced by his family for marrying a virtuous, lower-class lady (Saint John's mother).

in a chair with his eyes closed for ten minutes between surgeries. He always prayed before every surgery, often praying with his patients, even with those of other faiths. His patients experienced so much peace as he radiated Christ, the Divine Physician's peace.

But Vittorio did not let his prestigious job define him. He fully embraced being a husband and father, even if his medical career tied him up. Though he couldn't attend daily Mass because of his work duties, he prayed frequently. His favorite prayer was the Psalms, and hers was the Rosary. Rosalia passed on her Marian devotion to Vittorio. Although they had few moments to pray together because of Vittorio's work demands, they did pray the Psalms and Rosary together. These prayers sustained them through the trials of a somewhat difficult courtship and a very demanding career. Despite their trying schedules, Vittorio and Rosalia never missed Sunday Mass. Vittorio also loved to study Scripture. According to Dr. Solinas, Vittorio believed it was fundamental for a man to be the head of his family and to lead the family as seen throughout Scripture.

It's worth noting that their marriage, the final stage of courtship, experienced the cross of infertility and child loss. Vittorio and Rosalia could only have one natural son, whom they named Diego. They had a miscarriage prior to Diego's birth. Because Diego's pregnancy proved challenging on Rosalia's body, they felt God calling them to foster children. They adopted seven children, including some with special needs. The story behind one of their adopted children best manifests their Christian charity. One of Vittorio's coworkers, suffering from cancer, prayed that someone would look after her daughter, Alessandra, after she passed away. This was no small prayer since the young girl had Down syndrome. Vittorio prayed with Rosalia about this decision. He would not be impulsive. They prayed together, and they opened the Gospel to the words: "And he that shall receive one such little child in my name, receiveth me" (Matt. 18:5). And their decision was made. Vittorio told his coworker, who was on her death-bed, that he and his wife would raise Alessandra. Vittorio's coworker immediately sat up and made the sign of cross on both Vittorio and Rosalia's heads. She told them that they would be blessed forever for this undertaking.

In 1998, the fifty-four-year-old Vittorio passed away from a long battle with peritonitis (inflammation on the inside of the abdomen). He told his family on his deathbed, "Even if I had become famous, or if I were rich with many houses, what would it matter now? What am I bringing before God? I carry the love that we have given to every-one in my life."[318] Vittorio did just that, being married to Rosalia for twenty-seven blessed years and welcoming seven adopted children into his home, in addition to his own biological son. In heaven he would bring a lifetime of memories and love before the throne of God.

Vittorio is buried in his hospital's chapel where in his life he spent many hours praying. A white book lies on his grave, listing all the graces people have already received

---

[318] Christian Meert, "Saintly Parents Inspire Holy Children: Venerable Vittorio Trancanelli," December 4, 2021, https://agape catholicministries.info/family-life/title-saintly-parents-inspire-holy -children-venerable-vittorio-trancanelli/.

through his intercession. His colleague wrote the first words in the book: "Welcome back, Doc." It was as if Vittorio had never left the hospital.

Vittorio and Rosalia's marriage would not have happened without God's grace. Many obstacles were present from the start of their courtship. Perseverance and patience were key. One of the greatest mistakes some people make is ruling out a potential spouse immediately without getting to know the person, hence the importance of the various stages of courtship. Had Rosalia rashly ruled out Vittorio, she would have never married him. Marriage is a discernment process, not a split decision of meeting someone and then knowing within a few seconds whether this person is *the* one. Few people fall in love right away; it happens more often that couples fall in love over time and for a lifetime. In this way they allow God's love to radiate from their marriage like grace pouring out from the Eucharistic heart of Jesus. Venerable Vittorio's beatification process was opened in 2006.

Servant of God Chiara Corbella and Enrico Petrillo

Falling in love and riding off into the sunset is a beautiful thought, but it seems better suited for a Hollywood movie than a holy marriage. I believe that if the Lord could apply one of His parables to Chiara Corbella and Enrico Petrillo, it would be the parable of the sower (see Matt. 13). Their courtship was rocky at times but eventually found the rich soil of which Christ speaks.

Servant of God Chiara and Enrico met for the first time in the summer of 2002 while on pilgrimage to Medjugorje. Ironically, Enrico broke up with his girlfriend on the trip. According to their close friends Simone Troisi and Christiana Paccini,

> During a meal in the hotel, Enrico raised his eyes and saw Chiara coming toward him, toward the only seat available. Her beauty immediately impressed him. He felt that it would take little to fall in love with her. Chiara, looking at Enrico imagining that he was not alone, immediately thought: "Oh! This boy is mine"—in the sense of "he is for me." Enrico clarified later, "It was an intuition, and each of us had the same thought at the same time. It was a long road at the beginning—we gave each other the first kiss after five months. She had said no to so many suitors. She was waiting; she knew that the right one for her would come along." In fact Chiara had never dated anyone steadily before then. Enrico was twenty-three, and Chiara was eighteen. The day was August 2.[319]

Having lost his father unexpectedly when he was twenty-three, Enrico once said, "I had to learn to accept the fact that people you love might die at any time. This impeded me from loving her deeply."[320]

Breakups and makeups characterized their relationship. Once, Chiara went on vacation just so she could forget

---

[319] Troisi, *Chiara Corbella Petrillo*, 12–13.
[320] Troisi, 13.

about Enrico. After going on a vocational course in Assisi, Chiara reached out to Father Vito to become her spiritual director. Around the same time, Father Vito also became Enrico's spiritual director. After one of their breakups, Enrico visited Father Vito. The next day Father Vito went to see Chiara and challenged her stubbornness.

Over time, Enrico came to a revelation that many in the world ignore: "If you recognize that you can love only in God, you must love God more than your wife, more than your husband. If you look for consolation in the love of a person who is near you, you are taking the wrong path, because only the Lord can give you consolation; and then, if the Lord wishes, He gives you consolation through another person."[321]

Their friends also noticed a profound change in Chiara. Specifically, they said "she passed from thinking that she had the right to Enrico to the understanding that the other is a gift of God."[322] Chiara's spiritual director once related, "Chiara understood precisely during the engagement that if that was not her mission, if Enrico were not the person God had thought of for her, then he must let her go for the good of both of them."[323] Our Lord was sowing seeds of surrender into both of their hearts.

On a ten-day organized spiritual hike culminating on August 2, 2008, at the Portiuncula in Assisi, Enrico and Chiara realized that God wanted them to be a gift to one another. Through it all, Father Vito kept urging the couple

---

[321] Troisi, 16.
[322] Troisi, 19.
[323] Troisi, 19.

to pray for healing. According to Chiara, "On the sixth day of the walk, Enrico and I found ourselves walking together. He looked at me and said, 'Shall we get married?' I looked at him and said, 'Yes, Enri . . . Okay.' And I was thinking: 'But we broke up a week before the trip!' But he insisted: 'No, no. I am serious: shall we get married?' And I: 'Enri! Yes . . . Okay.' And I was thinking: 'This guy has sunstroke.'"[324]

After picking a sunflower, Enrico drew nearer to Chiara and said, "I am serious. Let's get married."[325] Chiara responded by saying "Okay!" But deep inside she pondered, "Who knows if he'll remember this tomorrow morning."[326] Chiara and Enrico were married less than two months later on September 21, 2008, in Assisi, with their spiritual director Father Vito by their side.

Chiara has been referred to as the "Second Saint Gianna" for refusing to abort her first two children even though she knew they would die shortly after birth from severe malformations. Chiara knew her children were a gift from God, even if her time with them was brief. She and Enrico were popular pro-life speakers, sharing their testimony of sacrifices made for their children.

During the pregnancy of her third child (Francesco, born healthy), the doctors found a massive tumor on her tongue. Again, Chiara was advised to abort her child, this time to save her own life. She refused this time too, and her son was born in May of 2011. Eventually her

---

[324] Troisi, 20.

[325] Troisi, 20.

[326] Troisi, 20.

cancer spread to the rest of her body. On June 13, 2012, Chiara died at the age of twenty-eight. She and Enrico had been married for just under four years. Overlooked in their suffering was Chiara and Enrico's beautiful but challenging courtship.

It is important to remember that even the holiest of marriages are not perfect. Some do not start off on good ground. At the same time, God often allows trials to test the seriousness of a couple's love. When Our Lord was explaining the parable of the sower, perhaps He was also describing certain courtships and marriages. In the end, Chiara and Enrico found the rich soil after Christ broke through their stony hearts, that is, their fears and stubbornness. Christ, the Master Gardener, tilled the rocky ground and sowed His seeds of virtue into their hearts. And though their marriage lasted briefly, this couple "brought forth fruit," by witnessing to everyone that marriage and human life are worth fighting for, even dying for (Matt. 13:8).

CONCLUSION

THE PEARL OF GREAT PRICE

"The kingdom of heaven is like to a merchant seeking good pearls. Who when he had found one pearl of great price, went his way, and sold all that he had, and bought it."

—Matthew 13:45–46

IN THE GOSPELS, Our Lord makes it clear that heaven is like a wedding banquet (see Matt. 22:1–14). In a similar way, courtship and marriage are likened to a man finding the pearl of great price, his calling to pursue one lady and risk everything for her. Notice the man does not find many pearls, but one. And this pearl will cost him everything: his time, his resources, but above all, his heart. Perhaps the merchant mentioned in the above Gospel passage must travel to the ends of the earth to find the esteemed pearl, and he will not give up until he finds his treasure. Similarly, some men spend years praying and searching to meet the woman God has chosen for them. And the same for some women who pray countless rosaries, novenas, and make holy hours, while patiently waiting for their prince to find them.

Of course, the pearl of great price has a deeper meaning, referring to Christ Himself. Just as saints like Benedict, Francis of Assisi, and Clare left everything behind to follow Christ, so too must a man leave behind all potential women for one woman—one who will be both his helpmate and his companion to heaven. Even more importantly, one whom he will sacrifice for, honor, and love every day of his life. She will call her husband to the heights of divine and human love. And he will do the same for his bride. Or, as Saint John Chrysostom explains best, "Young husbands should say to their wives: I have taken you in my arms, and I love you, and I prefer you to my life itself. For the present life is nothing, and my most ardent dream is to spend it with you in such a way that we may be assured of not being separated in the life reserved for us. . . . I place your love above all things, and nothing would be more bitter or painful to me than to be of a different mind than you."[327]

Perhaps this is one reason Saint Louis Martin came to his senses in his mid-thirties. He realized more than ever, especially after discerning he did not have a call to religious life, that he could not live for himself any longer as a single man. God was calling him to lay down his life by loving Saint Zélie more than himself. Here is the secret of happiness: self-forgetfulness, the martyrdom of one's will, and the desire to reach heaven. In both courtship and marriage, selfishness and happiness cannot coexist. In fact, no marriage can provide perfect happiness. Saints Louis and Zélie Martin and the couples listed in this book

---

[327] Cited in *CCC* 2365.

had one ultimate goal: to help their spouse and their children reach heaven, "for the present life is nothing, and my most ardent dream is to spend it with you" for all eternity.

A man can only find the pearl of great price, his future wife, if he first finds the Pearl of Great Price, Christ Himself. Only when a man finds Christ can he discover who he is and for whom he is being called to lay down his life. Christ is the love that every man and woman truly seeks, and it is His love and beauty that shines forth through all human love that is rooted in the Divine Love. So when these saintly couples fell in love, they drew their spouse and eventually their children to the source of their love: God Himself. Their love became swept up in the Trinitarian love, for every home is meant to be an earthly trinity where husband and wife pour out their love upon each other, spilling over to their children.

To marry a virtuous spouse is greater than any earthly treasure. As Proverbs declares, "Blessed is the man that findeth wisdom and is rich in prudence: The purchasing thereof is better than the merchandise of silver, and her fruit than the chiefest and purest gold: She is more precious than all riches: and all the things that are desired, are not to be compared with her" (Prov. 3:13–15). In fact, the Complete Jewish Bible says this woman "is more precious than pearls" (Prov. 3:15). For those called to marriage, finding a virtuous spouse is the greatest treasure outside of the Holy Eucharist. One's calling unlocks the meaning of one's existence and one's path to heaven.

Finding the virtues of Saint Joseph and Our Lady in your future spouse is indeed finding the pearl of great price. Once you find that pearl of virtue, you will leave everything behind for that person. You will forsake all other men and women to be with that one person until death. You will forsake your parents' home to cling to this person. You will leave behind all childish and empty pursuits to die to yourself for this one person. You will no longer live for yourself but for your spouse and, God willing, your future children.

Since these saintly couples knew that their purpose in life was to know, love, and serve God in this life in order to be happy with him in the next, they knew that marrying a godly spouse and growing in virtue with them was fundamental to reaching heaven. Hence, many of these couples, since their youth, strove to keep their "wedding garment" unstained through a life of purity, chastity, and frequent confession. They wanted to present themselves holy to God on their judgment day, but also to their spouse on their wedding night (see Matt. 22:11). In all things, the saints started with this end in mind: the Beatific Vision. During their courtships, they frequently asked this question: Will this person lead me to God?

Because God desires chaste courtships and faithful marriages, He longs for every couple to imitate His holy relatives: Boaz and Ruth, Joachim and Anne, Joseph and Mary. And He longs for couples to learn from His saints. The saints also desire for every couple to have holy and happy marriages with holy offspring. They also endured trials and were victorious with God's grace, and so can play a role in our victory as well. All of heaven is waiting to intervene. Saints Raphael, Padre Pio, Josemaría Escrivá, and Gianna Molla and others play special roles in assisting you in your courtship and marriage. Therefore, we must follow their example and ask for their intercession.

At the same time, all of hell wishes to destroy God's plan for marriage between one man and one woman through the fear of commitment and "postponed marriages," through unchaste courtships, through contraception, pornography, cohabitation, discord, infidelity, and, finally, divorce. While God and His saints are matchmakers, the devil is the diabolical divorcer who seeks to lead souls astray from a sacred marriage.

These marriage stories reveal another truth that many forget: the saints were the greatest lovers. Not only did they love God above everything, but they loved every person because each of us is made in His image and likeness. The married saints loved their spouses with a passion that the world has never seen before, a love that triumphs over the greatest love stories depicted in any movie, song, or novel. It was a love that led Saint Elizabeth of Hungary to run to her husband and "kiss him affectionally more than a thousand times on the mouth."[328] It was a love that led Saint Francis Borgia and Blessed Marcel Callo and so many saints to prepare for marriage with purity and chastity. It was a love that led Saint Gianna and Pietro Molla to write beautiful, romantic love letters to each other throughout their marriage. And it was a love that was ready to forgive any injury like Saint Rita and Blessed Elizabeth Mora. Contrary to

---

[328] Holböck, *Married Saints and Blesseds Through the Centuries*, 195.

common thought, the saints' love was not prudish or stiff, rather it was intensely passionate and joyful.

There is no such thing as "fate" or "serendipity" in God's eyes, only His providence. To find one's spouse, one begins with prayer, a life of virtue, avoiding sin, and waiting on the Lord and the saints to intervene. God desires that we have the closest union with Him and our spouse *now* as a preparation for our perpetual marriage in heaven with Him.

Just as Christ the King willingly lays down His life for His Bride, the Church, from His Eucharistic Throne, so must husbands do for their brides. And just as Mary the Queen humbly receives everything from Our Lord, so must wives act toward their husbands. If we live Christ's commands and love our spouse like He loves us, we shall proclaim, "For a day in thy courts is better than a thousand elsewhere" (Ps 84:10, RSV). From the shores of heaven, the saints are cheering, interceding, and reminding us that, "We are born to love, we live to love, and we will die to love still more."[329]

---

[329] "Saints of the Day-Joseph Cafasso," CatholicSaints.Info, catholic saints.info/saints-of-the-day-joseph-cafasso/.

PART II

COURTSHIP COUNSEL & PRAYERS

HOW TO CHOOSE
A SPOUSE[330]

THE FOLLOWING QUESTIONS will not only help you to fit yourself for leading a worthy and holy married life, but also enable you to choose a spouse in marriage intelligently. These qualifications apply to men and women alike.

I. FRIENDSHIP

1. Is your friendship morally beneficial? Are you morally better or worse for having been with him, and what can you expect in the future? Would marriage with him help you to observe God's commandments and practice your religious duties faithfully?

2. Imagine a crisis in your life (poverty, sickness) that might demand a high quality of virtue to remain faithful to God. Would he be a help to the practice of such virtue?

3. Does he drink too much? Gamble?

---

[330] The following section was taken from Lawrence G. Lovasik's *Clean Love in Courtship*, 62–66. Used with permission from TAN Books.

4. Does he want to indulge in petting, passionate kissing, even at the expense of chastity?
5. Does he control his temper? Has he a sense of humor? Can he keep a secret?
6. Does he practice his religion?
7. What are his views on divorce, on having children, on Catholic education, on frequenting the sacraments?
8. Can you actually point out any definite virtuous qualities, or are they put on for your benefit now?

II. AGREEMENT

1. Is there at least a reasonable degree of similarity between you in regard to the recreations you like?
2. Could you both enjoy staying at home in the evening, especially when children come?
3. Are there any habits now that not only get on your nerves but which you find extraordinarily difficult to overlook?
4. Do you both fit into about the same kind of social life?
5. Does he get along with your family and you with his?
6. Have you both sufficient health for marriage?
7. What are his habits of life: cleanliness, orderliness, good manners, good grammar?
8. Are you able to harmonize judgments on things that pertain to family life: food, kind of house, furnishings, etc.?

9. Have you the same religion and the same standards concerning its practice?
10. Have you the same attitude toward children and their education?
11. Do you feel at ease together, regardless of what you talk about? If you do not meet for some time, are you able to take up where you left off, with something of the naturalness of a family reunion, or do you have to try to work up an acquaintance all over again?
12. Has he a nagging or reforming disposition?
13. Do you see his failings, and are you willing to tolerate them? Does he admit them, and is he willing to get over them?
14. With children in mind, would you say that this person would be just the right other parent for them?

III. SELF-SACRIFICE

1. Is your prospective companion thoughtful of others and has he the power of self-discipline?
2. In his home does he show thoughtfulness of parents and brothers and sisters, and do you get the impression that this is his regular attitude?
3. What little kindnesses, not only to you but to others, have you noticed in him?
4. When he is wrong, does he admit it and try to make up for it?

5. Does he easily and graciously pass over others' mistakes?
6. Does he look for sympathy too much?
7. Can he give sympathy willingly, or does someone else's trouble always bring out a greater trouble of his?
8. Does he show that he knows his temper and that jealousy and other unpleasant traits ought to be controlled?

IF IT IS A WIFE YOU WANT:

1. Can she cook and make the house a home?
2. Has she that womanly quality that instinctively puts things in order?
3. Would this girl be a real mother?
4. Could she bear children and sacrifice for them?
5. Could she give the child that early introduction to God that he would never forget?
6. Is she convinced that motherhood is an all-day and an all-night job?
7. How does she speak of children? How does she treat them?
8. What do her younger brothers and sisters think of her?

IF IT IS A HUSBAND YOU WANT:

1. How does he like children?
2. Does he like to work? Can he hold a job?
3. Has he a sense of responsibility?

4. Is he "grown up," or does he have to be pampered?
5. Is he unduly jealous? A braggart? An alibi-artist?
   Is he courteous?

Such questions will bring you down-to-earth and keep you from estimating things merely on the score of fascination. Many of the points are not in themselves important; the general picture that is created by the various answers is very important. Many points cannot be tested out before marriage, but glaring risks can be easily recognized. Though these characteristics need not be present in a high degree at the time of marriage, the beginnings should be present, or at least a genuine willingness and effort to improve.

If there is question of reforming your friend, it should be done before, not after, marriage. Do not put your faith in vague promises which seldom materialize. If you cannot get along agreeably before marriage, it is almost certain that you will not get along after marriage.

As soon as you have finally resolved to accept one another as mates, if no insurmountable hindrance is in the way, consult your pastor and set the date for your marriage. You should derive a certain satisfaction from the publication of the banns of marriage because you have nothing to be ashamed of.

Before marriage pay close attention to the instruction on marriage and its ethics given you by the priest. Read a popular and practical treatise on the subject. It may be advisable to make a general confession before entering the holy state of marriage. Penance is a second baptism. It will gratify you to know that you are beginning married life with a soul entirely free from every stain of sin. This is absolutely necessary for those who have sinned in court-ship and have been receiving the Sacraments unworthily in consequence, lest they receive Matrimony sacrilegiously and thus be bereft of its graces. Arrange for a devotional and inspiring church wedding with Holy Mass and the special blessing of God and of the Church. It will always be a beautiful and heartening memory for life.

FOR THOSE DISCERNING MARRIAGE

PRAY: YOU WILL never have this much free time in your life for prayer unless you become a priest or join a religious order. Develop your prayer life. Set aside at least twenty minutes a day for mental prayer. Attend daily Mass as often as possible and weekly adoration. Build that foundation that will support you throughout your marriage. Pray a "Hail Mary," or some prayer each day for your spouse. Pray that God may keep your future spouse from serious sin along with yourself.

Be holy now: The best way to live the married vocation is to be holy now. If you are struggling with lust, perhaps pornography, seek help, sometimes even professional help. Marriage will not cure your lust. The sins you commit will likely be passed onto your children. Put on that armor now as Saint Paul says. Seek the sacraments frequently and devoutly, seek Our Lady's help in the Rosary. With God's grace, you will slowly root out all mortal sin, and slowly combat many venial sins.

Be courageous: Every time that you say "no" to impurity is a "yes" to your future spouse. Stay committed to present that most splendid rose, that is, your virginity, to your spouse on your wedding night rather than one with only a few petals. Even though the culture tells us to "show off" through revealing clothes, strive to dress modestly. Yoga pants will not get you a godly man. Wearing sleeveless shirts to display your muscles could turn off a virtuous woman.

Live now: Live your vocation now. God is calling you to live your single vocation generously. Use your time wisely and live for others. Consider visiting a nursing home, praying in front of an abortion clinic, serving at a homeless shelter, or babysitting a married friend's children so that they can have a date night. You are not guaranteed to be alive five years from now or even tomorrow.

Cultivate your mind: Read good novels, spiritual reading, especially solid books and podcasts on dating and purity by Jason and Crystalina Evert and visit their website at chastity.com. Father Lawrence G. Lovasik's short book, *Clean Love in Courtship*, published by TAN Books, is a classic. Father Thomas Morrow's book, *Christian Courtship in an Oversexed World: A Guide for Catholics*, is another great one.

Avoid busyness: While your work is important, it is not the reason for your existence. Many young men and women are so absorbed and burned out from their work that they turn down many suitors' requests for a coffee date.

Stay fit: Just as the male cardinal allures the opposite sex by its colors, so also a well-kept body can help you not only release tension but make you more attractive to your future spouse. Commit yourself to exercising a few times a week. At the same time, don't overdo it. If you work out more than you pray, you are out of balance. Exercise is also crucial for your mental health.

Embrace suffering: Understand that you will get rejected at times. Understand that it might take years before you are asked out on a date. Take comfort in the fact that Jesus was also rejected and abandoned by His closest friends. Draw nearer to the cross. When choosing a spouse, look for someone who knows how to handle suffering well.

Develop new talents and have fun: Perhaps you have always wanted to play an instrument or learn how to watercolor. Now is your chance. Don't waste your life waiting for things to happen; rather, spend your life making things happen. Blessed Pier Giorgio Frassati was fond of rock climbing, smoking cigars, and skiing. Have some fun. God didn't create you to sulk in your misery.

Discipline and moderation: The habits you form now will spill over to marriage. If you spend hours on social media, then this will likely continue into your marriage. Your spouse and children should never have to compete with technology. They want real "facetime" with you. If you love to drink and eat lavishly, this too will need to be curbed. If you love to stay up late and wake up around noon, you are in for a big surprise. Start preparing yourself now for marriage.

Financial stability: Most couples getting married will have some debt, such as student loans. But that should be the only debt. Today, there is no such thing as a dowry. In many cases, spouses will bring debt. One also cannot put off marriage because one doesn't have enough saved to purchase a house or because of many student loans. Debt, as I like to call it, refers to the **D**evil's **E**vil **B**ank & **T**rust. Financial problems cause many headaches in marriage. Start saving now and being wise, but at the same time be generous where you can.

Friendship dating: Don't be afraid to ask someone to meet you for coffee. A woman should not be afraid to say "no" if he asks for a second date, especially if he only cares about her body or shows no interest in her Faith. In friendship dating, "you just get together as friends once a week or so, for one to three months with no kissing. A chaste hug, yes, but no romantic words, no hand-holding, no commitment," according to Father Thomas Morrow.[331] Never settle for a mediocre person. Be a missionary, but don't do missionary dating, because only God can change a heart.

Find community: Join your diocese's young adult group, attend Theology on Tap talks, join a local meetup group. You will be more likely to find a godly spouse here than at a bar or some club.

Be realistic: While you should be attracted to your spouse, not everyone can marry Mr. Darcy or some supermodel. Not everyone can marry Saint Joseph or Our Lady. Virtue, especially one's faith in God, is of extreme

---

[331] Morrow, *Christian Courtship in an Oversexed World*, 93–94.

importance; but also understand that your spouse will never be perfect. Understand that your spouse will never fulfill all the desires of your heart—only God can. Your spouse can never take the place of God. At the same time, we must never forget the Reverend Mother's timeless words to Maria in *The Sound of Music*: "My daughter, if you love this man, it doesn't mean you love God less." Loving God and our future spouse is not a question of "either/ or," but really "both/and."

Seek counseling: Perhaps your parents' divorce, even a past sexual or emotional wound, or pain inflicted by others has hurt you, sometimes unconsciously. If you have been scarred, then seek healing before you enter marriage. You are not your parents' past failed marriage or the sum of your past sins or the abuse that others have inflicted on you.

Be joyful: Look for someone who is joyful. A negative person, one who complains, especially about suffering and setbacks, might not be the best fit. And if you are prone to negativity, work on it. Ask the Holy Spirit to flood your soul with His peace and joy. Our joy is not contingent upon our circumstances, but is a fruit of the Holy Spirit (see Gal. 5:22).

Trust: Most of all, let go of all anxiety and be at peace. God is in control. God cares more about introducing you to your spouse than you do. Eve didn't scout the ends of the world for Adam nor Adam for Eve. God brought Eve to Adam.[332] And if God doesn't introduce you to your spouse, it is because He has someone better for you: Himself.

---

[332] I am thankful to Kimberly Hahn for this insight.

Gratitude: Blessed Solanus Casey used to say, "Thank God ahead of time."[333] Thank God for His many gifts and His many trials. God is giving you everything you need to become a saint. Thank Him now for your future spouse should He wish to bestow that gift upon you. Each night, thank Him for at least one blessing and even one cross, for everything comes from His hands.

Seek the saints and angels: The saints and angels in heaven are very much concerned with your vocation, especially your guardian angel. Start a novena to your favorite saint, but also resign yourself to the reality that God's timing is everything. Remember that the goal of prayer is to draw near to God and to conform our will to His.

---

[333] "Thank God Ahead of Time," Solanus Casey Center, November 23, 2015, solanuscenter.org/about-us/blog/thank-god-ahead-of-time.

FOR THE MARRIED COUPLE

REMEMBER: REDISCOVER WHY you fell in love in the first place and continue to fall in love. Don't let the fire burn out. You cannot know everything about your spouse on your wedding day. Let his or her life unfold. Study your spouse and ask him or her questions. Share your dreams, your desires, your sufferings. Intimacy takes a lifetime. Most of all, a husband ought to pursue his wife "until death do you part." Don't let your anniversary and Valentine's Day be the only days you do something special for your bride; you should do something every day to make your spouse feel appreciated. And one of the best ways to remember your "why" is to write down your marriage story, that is, how and where you met your spouse and why you fell in love. Give a copy to your children and grandchildren some-day. Read your marriage story on your anniversary, but especially when your marriage is going through difficult times. Our love for our spouse can easily become luke-warm when we forget God's blessings, when we forget the miracle of falling in love and staying in love.

Weekly date night and romance (at home): This can be as simple as having a glass of wine together, watching a movie, and cuddling on the couch.

Monthly date night (outside the home): It is important to get out of the house even if it is for an hour or so. You can even swap free babysitting service with some trusty friends or find a good sitter in the neighborhood or hire a teenage girl from church who has ten younger siblings. You don't always have to spend money. Sometimes just going for a walk at a park can be beautiful. After all, someday it will be just you and your spouse when the kids leave the house. The way you love your spouse often sets up your children's future marriages for success or failure. And, yes, you must love your spouse more than your children, but not more than God.

Exercise and eat healthy: Take care of your body to ensure a longer life with your spouse and children. You also want to look good for your spouse. Although you will probably never look as good or as slim as you did on your wedding day, it is important to stay fit for your spouse. Imagine going to Mass on Sunday with shabby clothes, your hair unkempt, and no makeup on. You are sending a message to God that you don't really care about Him because you don't care about yourself. The healthier and more fit you look will also make you more attractive to your spouse. So, dress nicely not just for God, but also for your spouse. If you are a woman, put on some makeup from time to time. If you are a man, look sharp for your wife. Go for walks with your spouse. Work out together if you can. If you eat healthier, you will not only feel better but look better.

Great spiritual friends: While you ought to be very close with your spouse, it is important to have at least one good friend of the same sex. It is better to have a handful of genuine friends than a thousand virtual friends online. It is important to talk with these friends and meet with them to build you up. God put them in your life for a reason. Spouses should encourage each other to get out of the house at least monthly to meet a friend or have a women's or men's night.

Laugh together: Marriage is filled with many crosses. During our pain, we must never forget to laugh often. Should God bless us with children, they will provide free comedy. We must also laugh at ourselves and never take ourselves or our spouse too seriously. Our spouse is not our savior but our companion.

Words and signs of affection: Give your spouse at least one compliment a day and truly mean it. Never cease telling him or her how much you love them. Give them an unexpected kiss or a massage. Ingratitude cools the flames of love while gratitude keeps the embers of love burning. For those couples blessed with children, it is crucial to show affection to your children, even as your children age. Teenager daughters who never get a hug from their father are more likely to seek affection in the wrong places.

Ask for forgiveness: If we expect God to forgive us, then we must forgive our spouse. And most of all, we must ask for forgiveness when we have hurt them. "I am sorry. I will do better next time." We need to hear the words from our spouse as much as Our Lord says to us in the sacrament of confession, "I forgive you."

Be humble and meek: The humble couple knows the truth about themselves. Therefore, they are not afraid of their wretchedness. They know they are imperfect, but they still seek God, who is perfect. They are not surprised by their failures, sins, and weaknesses. And they are quick to ask for forgiveness when they make mistakes and to grant forgiveness when their spouse or children mess up. They do not return injury for injury. They seek to bear the injustices that come their way even if they did nothing wrong.

Be positive: Just as negativity and complaining are contagious, so is being positive. Don't let negativity permeate your house. Always give your spouse the benefit of the doubt.

Sacrifice joyfully and invisibly: The most meritorious acts are those done when no one is looking or those done voluntarily without even being asked. We do them out of love and not to be thanked. Countless opportunities await, such as dirty dishes in the sink, clothes to be folded, etc.

Pray together: The greatest act a couple can do together is not going shopping, snorkeling, or watching TV together, but praying together. The more you love God, the more you will love your spouse. Go to Eucharistic Adoration together. Pray a Rosary together when you can. Read a spiritual book together. Go to confession together. Set some time for just the two of you to pray together. Pray for your children and most of all for each other. Also realize you are not your spouse's spiritual director. The more we love God, the more patient we will be with our spouse and our children. God wants you, your spouse, and children in heaven more than you do, but we must respond to His graces.

Pray alone: Every husband and wife must make time for private prayer, such as twenty minutes a day for silence. This is usually best first thing in the morning before the children wake up. Go on a yearly retreat, and, if possible, schedule a weekly or monthly holy hour just by yourself. Pray more for your spouse than you pray for yourself.

Know thy enemy: You and your spouse are on the same team, though sometimes it may not seem that way. The real enemy is Satan, who seeks to destroy your marriage. He incites you to fight and to disagree with your spouse. He whispers lies about your spouse.

Be a saint: The best way for a marriage to grow is if you strive to become a saint. We cannot expect others to be holy, especially our spouse, if we are not willing to lead the way. God leads every person on a different spiritual journey. Become holy and see how God uses you to bring others with you. A rich sacramental life is the key, such as monthly confession and Mass every Sunday and holy day along with daily Mass if your schedule allows it. We need God's grace to achieve any good in our lives.

BE APOSTLES
TO SINGLES

INVITE: IT IS easy to forget about your single friends when you are married. Often when a man or woman gets married, their former friendships can fade, especially with their single friends, sadly, even with their own siblings. Although your spouse and children must be placed before your friends, it is important not to forget them. Invite them for dinner occasionally, if they live in the area, or meet them at the park. Call them when it is on your heart, especially on their birthdays. Don't forget that when you got married, they lost a part of you. And, though your friendship may not be the same, it can remain strong if you stay connected. Being around you and your family might inspire or deter them from the married vocation depending on how well you live your vocation. Be a great witness to them! They might even enjoy watching your kids.

Encourage: Many single friends can lose hope after years of not going on a date or never meeting a good Catholic; discouragement sets in. And, as a result, they begin to believe lies about themselves, "Maybe I am not good enough. Maybe I am not attractive enough. Maybe God doesn't have a plan for my life." Consequently, many can find themselves tempted by various sexual sins, such as pornography or hooking up. Even worse, they might want to give up on their Faith. Be the voice of Christ by telling these single souls to keep praying, hoping, and trying. Tell them they are beautiful and that God has great plans for them. Let them know you are always there for them should they need you.

Introduce: Although not everyone feels comfortable doing this, think about connecting your single friend to another single friend, especially if both persons love their Faith and share the same values. Many marriages have resulted from a simple introduction. If the Holy Spirit is nudging you, follow His prompting even if nothing transpires. Also, ask your friend first. Some people prefer to take matters in their own hands.

Pray: Above all, pray for your single brothers and sisters in Christ that God's peace may guide them in the present moment. Pray that they may live their single vocation joyfully. And pray for their perseverance to keep going, especially on Saint Valentine's Day and other days that might be difficult for them. Offer your Rosary or Mass intentions for them, so that they can live a chaste and pure life as they prepare for their vocation.

PRAYERS

MORNING PRAYER TO THE BLESSED MOTHER[334]

Mary, loving Daughter of God the Father, I give my soul to your care. Protect the life of God in my soul; do not let me lose it by serious sin. Protect my mind and my will, so that all my thoughts and desires will be pleasing to God.

Hail Mary, full of grace . . .

Mary, loving Mother of God the Son, I give my heart to your care. Let me love Jesus with all my heart. Let me always try to love my neighbor, and let me avoid friends who might lead me away from Jesus and into a life of sin.

Hail Mary, full of grace . . .

Mary, loving Spouse of the Holy Spirit, I give my body to your care. Let me always remember that my body is a home for the Holy Spirit, Who dwells in me. Let me never sin against Him by any impure actions, alone or with others, against the virtue of purity.

---

[334] This devotion is prayed daily to Our Lady, preferably in the morning, asking protection from sin, especially all mortal sin. I am grateful to the late Father Andrew Apostoli, CFR, for introducing me to this prayer. Various saints like Leonard of Port-Maurice and Alphonsus de Liguori recommended saying three Hail Mary's in the morning and evening to remain in a state of grace.

Hail Mary, full of grace . . .

A Prayer for Daily Neglects[335]

Eternal Father, I offer Thee the Sacred Heart of Jesus, with all its love, all its sufferings and all its merits.

First: To expiate all the sins I have committed this day and during all my life.

Glory Be . . .

Second: To purify the good I have done poorly this day and during all my life.

Glory Be . . .

Third: To supply for the good I ought to have done, and that I have neglected this day and during all my life.

Glory Be . . .

Prayer to Saint Raphael for the Wise Choice of a Marriage Partner[336]

O Glorious Saint Raphael, Patron and Lover of the Young, I call upon thee and plead with thee for thy help. In all confidence I open my heart to thee, to beg thy guidance and assistance in the important task of planning my future. Obtain for me through thy intercession the light of God's grace, so that I may decide wisely concerning the person who is to be my partner through life. O Angel of Happy

---

[335] Cruz, *Prayers and Heavenly Promises*, 4.
[336] "Prayer to St. Raphael for the Wise Choice of a Marriage Partner," BeautySoAncient, www.beautysoancient.com/prayer-to-st-raphael-for-the-wise-choice-of-a-marriage-partner/.

Meetings, lead us by the hand to find each other. May all our movements be guided by thy light and transfigured by thy joy. As thou didst lead the young Tobias to Sara and opened up for him a new life of happiness with her in holy marriage, lead me to such a one whom in thine angelic wisdom thou dost judge best suited to be united with me in marriage.

Saint Raphael, loving patron of those seeking a marriage partner, help me in this supreme decision of my life. Find for me as a helpmate in life that person whose character will reflect the traits of Jesus and Mary. May he (she) be upright, loyal, pure, sincere and noble, so that with united efforts and with chaste and unselfish love, we both may strive to perfect ourselves in soul and body, as well as the children it may please God to entrust to our care.

Saint Raphael, Angel of chaste courtship, bless our friendship and our love, that sin may have no part in it. May our mutual love bind us so closely that our future home may ever be most like the home of the Holy Family of Nazareth. Offer thy prayers to God for both of us and obtain the blessing of God upon our marriage, as thou wert the herald of blessing for the marriage of Tobias and Sara.

Saint Raphael, friend of the young, be thou my friend, for I shall always be thine. I desire to ever invoke thee in my needs. To thy special care I entrust the decision I am to make as to my future wife (husband). Direct me to the person with whom I can best cooperate in doing God's Holy Will, with whom I can live in peace, love and harmony in this life and attain eternal joy in the next. Amen.

PRAYER FOR A GOOD HUSBAND OR WIFE[337]

O Jesus, the dearest Friend I have, in all confidence I open my heart to You to beg Your light and assistance in the important task of planning my future. Give me the light of Your grace, that I may decide wisely concerning the person who is to be my spouse through life. Dearest Jesus, send me such a one whom in Your divine wisdom You judge best suited to be united with me in marriage. May her/his character reflect some of the traits of Your own Sacred Heart. May he/she be upright, loyal, pure, sincere and noble, so that with united efforts and with pure and unselfish love we both may strive to perfect ourselves in soul and body, as well as the children it may please You to entrust to our care. Bless our friendship before marriage, that sin may have no part in it. May our mutual love bind us so closely that our future home may ever be most like Your own at Nazareth.

O Mary Immaculate, sweet Mother, to your special care I entrust the decision I am to make as to my future wife/husband. You are my guiding Star! Direct me to the person with whom I can best cooperate in doing God's Holy Will, with whom I can live in peace, love and harmony in this life, and attain to eternal joys in the next. Amen.

---

[337] "Prayer for a Good Husband or Wife," Powerful Catholic Prayers, powerfulcatholicprayers.com/prayer-good-husband-wife/. This prayer was modified.

PRAYER TO SAINT JOSEPH AND OUR LADY TO KNOW MY VOCATION
BY PATRICK O'HEARN

Saint Joseph, virginal father of Jesus, intercede that I may know and do God's will like you did on earth by responding to the vocation God has planted in my heart from all eternity. Help me to be courageous, pure, and holy, just like you. Help me never to count the cost, but to die to myself daily as you did.

Our Lady, spouse of the Holy Spirit, intercede that I may follow God's will like you did on earth by saying "Yes," to God even though I do not know what path lies ahead. Help me to trust God wholeheartedly without anxiety and fear, so that I may be happy in this life and for all eternity.

I ask this in the name of your Son, Jesus Christ, Our Lord.

Amen.

MEMORARE
BY SAINT BERNARD OF CLAIRVAUX
(FOR ONE'S FUTURE SPOUSE)

Remember,
O most gracious Virgin Mary,
that never was it known that anyone who fled to thy protection,
implored thy help, or sought thy intercession,
was left unaided.
Inspired by this confidence,
I fly unto thee,

O Virgin of virgins, my Mother;
to thee do I come,
before thee I stand,
sinful and sorrowful;
O Mother of the Word Incarnate,
despise not my petitions,
but in thy mercy hear and answer me.
Amen.

Prayer to my Guardian Angel
by Patrick O'Hearn

O Guardian Angel, ever present at my side since my conception, help me to follow the path that God is calling me to. If I am called to marriage, keep me pure as you are pure. Help me to love God as you do. Intercede for my future spouse that he/she too might be pure and holy.

Through your prayers and protection, lead me to my spouse.

Amen.

SAINTLY SAYINGS

"It seems you're still thinking of Mademoiselle X? I think you're foolish. . . . I can't stop thinking about it. You're going to hurt yourself, either with her or with someone else, because you only consider the superficial things, beauty and wealth, without worrying about the qualities that make a husband happy or the faults that cause him grief and ruin. You know all that glitters is not gold. The main thing is to look for a good woman whose interests center on the home, who is not afraid of dirtying her hands with work, who devotes time to her appearance only as much as she has to, and who knows how to raise children to work and be holy. A woman like that would scare you; she would not be brilliant enough in the eyes of world. But sensible people would love her better even if she had nothing, rather than another woman with a dowry of fifty thousand francs and who lacked these qualities." [338]

—Saint Zélie Martin

"Every man who pursues a maid, every maid who yearns to be courted, every bond of friendship in the universe, seeks a love that is not just her love or his love but something that overflows

---

[338] Martin, *A Call to a Deeper Love*, 11. Saint Zélie Martin wrote the above words to her younger brother, Isidore. These profound words ought to be heeded by every man looking to marry.

both her and him which is called "our love." Everyone is in love with an ideal love, a love that is so far beyond sex that sex is forgotten. We all love something more than we love. When that overflow ceases, love stops. As the poet puts it: 'I could not love thee, dear, so much, loved I not honour more.' That ideal love we see beyond all creature-love, to which we instinctively turn when flesh-love fails, is the same ideal that God had in His Heart from all eternity—the Lady whom He calls 'Mother.' She is the one whom every man loves when he loves a woman— whether he knows it or not. She is what every woman wants to be when she looks at herself. She is the woman whom every man marries in ideal when he takes a spouse."[339]

—Venerable Fulton J. Sheen

"Faithfulness in Christian marriage entails that: great mortification. For a Christian man there is no escape. Marriage may help to sanctify & direct to its proper object his sexual desires; its grace may help him in the struggle; but the struggle remains. It will not satisfy him—as hunger may be kept off by regular meals. It will offer as many difficulties to its purity proper to that state, as it provides easements. No man, however truly he loved his betrothed and bride as a young man, has lived faithful to her as a wife in mind and body without deliberate conscious exercise of the will, without self-denial. Too few are told that—even those brought up 'in the Church'. Those outside seem seldom to have heard it."[340]

—J. R. R. Tolkien

---

[339] Sheen, *The World's First Love*, 12–13.
[340] Tolkien, *The Letters of J.R.R. Tolkien*, 51.

"I have spent almost forty years preaching the vocational meaning of marriage. More than once I have had occasion to see faces light up as men and women, who had thought that in their lives a dedication to God was incompatible with a noble and pure human love, heard me say that marriage is a divine path on earth!"[341]

—Saint Josemaría Escrivá

"Let us then trust ourselves entirely to God and His Providence and leave Him complete power to order our lives, turning to Him lovingly in every need and awaiting His help without anxiety. Leave everything to Him and He will provide us with everything, at the time and in the place and in the manner best suited. He will lead us on our way to that happiness and peace of mind for which we are destined in this life as a foretaste of the everlasting happiness we have been promised."[342]

—Saint Claude de la Colombière, SJ

"If you have always loved, prized and guarded purity and innocence as your most precious personal possession, your wedding day will be a truly happy day. If you have prepared for marriage by a courtship characterized from beginning to end by a high mutual esteem, ideal love and devotion, angelic purity and unfailing self-restraint, begotten by the fear as well as the love of the Lord and a tender, reverential regard for one another, then you will taste the sweetest

---

[341] Escrivá de Balaguer. *Conversations with Saint Josemaría Escrivá*, No. 91.
[342] Saint-Jure, *Trustful Surrender to Divine Providence*, 128–29.

happiness that God grants to man in this vale of tears when the priest binds you in the deathless union of the Sacrament of Matrimony."[343]

—Father Lawrence G. Lovasik, SVD

"You husbands and fathers say that you love your wives and children. Ok, I am going to take you seriously. Now if you love them really (that is, for their genuine welfare and not simply for what you can get from them, or whether they do or do not return your love as you would like it to be returned)—I repeat, if you love them really, then prove it in the best way possible: become a saint, get rid of your faults, love totally. Why is this the best thing you can do for them? Your impact for their genuine, eternal welfare will be tremendous. Yes, you also show love for wife and children by putting bread on the table and a roof over their heads, but the best proof of genuine love is found in the example of an exemplary life: a tremendous spur to their eternal enthrallment, and yours as well."[344]

—Father Thomas Dubay, SM

"You say you love your husband and children; then prove it in the best way possible: become a saintly wife, a saintly mother, etc."[345]

—Father Thomas Dubay, SM

---

[343] Lovasik, *Clean Love in Courtship*, 69
[344] Dubay, *Deep Conversion, Deep Prayer*, 60–61.
[345] Dubay, 61.

CONTEMPLATIVE QUESTIONS

1. How do I pray daily for my future spouse?
2. What saints and angels can I invoke to intercede for my future marriage?
3. Was there ever a time I felt an angel leading me to do something or meet someone?
4. When I am discouraged by not meeting my spouse, what actions can I take?
5. In what places should I look for my spouse?
6. What risks am I willing to take to meet my spouse?
7. What obstacles stand in the way of me pursuing a spouse?
8. What virtues can I work on before getting married?
9. What areas of my life do I need God to heal before getting married and who can help me with those?
10. What are the qualities that I look for in my spouse? If I am married, what "greater qualities" do I notice in them now (as Venerable Fulton Sheen said)?
11. What are the nonnegotiables that my spouse must have?
12. How much time should pass before I know my spouse is the one?

13. If I am married, how can I rekindle my love?
14. If I am married, what are some practical steps I can take to grow in union with God and my spouse?

BIBLIOGRAPHY

Agreda, Mary of. *The Mystical City of God. A Popular Abridgement of the Divine History and Life of the Virgin Mother of God*. Translated by Fiscar Marison (Rev. Geo. J. Blatter). Charlotte, NC: TAN Books, 2012.

Allen, Diane. *Pray, Hope, and Don't Worry: True Stories of Padre Pio Book 1*. Seattle, WA: Padre Pio Press, 2013.

Bailey, Beth L. *From Front Porch to Back Seat: Courtship in Twentieth-Century America*. Baltimore, MD: The John Hopkins University Press, 1989.

Bennett, Art and Laraine. *The Temperament God Gave You: The Classic Key to Knowing Yourself, Getting Along with Others, and Growing Closer to God*. Manchester, NH: Sophia Institute, 2005.

Beretta, Gianna and Pietro Molla. *The Journey of Our Love: The Letters of Saint Gianna Beretta and Pietro Molla*. Edited by Elio Guerriero. Boston: Pauline Books & Media, 2014.

Bessières, Albert. *Wife, Mother and Mystic (Blessed Anna-Maria Taigi)*. Translated by Stephen Rigby. Charlotte, NC: TAN Books, 1970.

Brown, Anne. *No Greater Love. Bl. Gianna Beretta Molla: Physician, Mother, Martyr*. New Hope, KY: New Hope Publications, 1999.

Burns, Paul. *Butler's Lives of the Saints: The Third Millennium.* London, UK: Burns & Oates, 2005.

Clarke, A. M. *The Life of St. Francis Borgia.* London: Burns and Oates, Limited, 1894.

Crosby, Michael, ed. *Solanus Casey: The Official Account of a Virtuous American Life.* New York: Cross Road Pub., 2000.

Cruz, Joan Carroll. *Prayers and Heavenly Promises.* Charlotte, NC: TAN Books, 1990

———. *Saintly Women of Modern Times.* Charlotte, NC: TAN Books, 2016.

Dubay, Thomas. *Deep Conversion, Deep Prayer.* San Francisco: Ignatius Press, 2006.

Emmerich, Anne Catherine. *The Life of Jesus Christ and Biblical Revelations, Volume I.* Gastonia, NC: TAN Books, 2021.

Escrivá de Balaguer, Josemaría, *Conversations with Saint Josemaría Escrivá.* No. 91. New York: Scepter, 2007.

Eymard, Saint Peter Julian. *The Real Presence: Eucharistic Meditations.* New York: Sentinel Press, 1938.

Frossard, André and John Paul II. *"Be Not Afraid!" Pope John Paul II Speaks Out on his Life, his Beliefs, and his Inspiring Vision for Humanity.* Translated by J. R. Foster. New York: St. Martin's Press, 1984.

Gihr, Nicholas. *The Holy Sacrifice of the Mass: Dogmatically, Liturgically and Ascetically Explained.* St. Louis, MO: B. Herder Co., 1933.

Herbert, Mary Elizabeth, *Life of the Venerable Elizabeth Canori Mora.* London: R. Washbourne, 1878.

Holböck, Ferdinand. *Married Saints and Blesseds Through the Centuries.* Translated by Michael J. Miller. San Francisco: Ignatius Press, 2002.

John of the Cross, Saint. *The Collected Works of St. John of the Cross*. Translated by Kieran Kavanaugh and Otilo Rodriguez. Washington, D.C.: ICS Publications, 1991.

John Paul II, Pope. *Gift and Mystery*. New York: Image Books, 1996.

Kindziuk, Milena. *Emilia I Karol Wojtylowie: Rodzice sw. Jana Pawla*. Krakow: Wydawnictwo Espirit, 2020.

Lovasik, Lawrence G, SVD. *Clean Love in Courtship*. Charlotte, NC: TAN Books, 1974.

Martin, Saint Zelie and Saint Louis Martin. *A Call to a Deeper Love*. Edited by Frances Renda and translated by Ann Connors Hess. Staten Island, NY: St. Paul's, 2011.

Molla, Pietro and Elio Guerriero. *Saint Gianna Molla: Wife, Mother, Doctor*. Translated by James G. Colbert. San Francisco: Ignatius Press, 2004.

Monti, James. *The King's Good Servant But God's First*. San Francisco: Ignatius Press, 1997.

Morrow, T. G. *Christian Courtship in an Oversexed World: A Guide for Catholics*. Huntington, IN: Our Sunday Visitor, 2003.

Munk, Barbara. *From the youth to the holiness [Od młodości, do świętości]*. Kraków, Poland. The Institute of Intercultural Dialogue dedicated to John Paul, 2016.

O'Hearn, Patrick. *Parents of the Saints: The Hidden Heroes Behind Our Favorite Saints*. Gastonia, NC: TAN Books, 2021.

Pastoral Constitution on the Church in the Modern World: *Gaudium et spes*. Promulgated by Pope Paul VI. Vatican City: 1965. Accessed October 10, 2018. http:vatican.va.

Pelucchi, Giuliana. *Saint Gianna: Her Life of Joy and Heroic Sac-rifice.* Translated by Michael J. Miller. Boston, MA: Pauline Books & Media, 2019.

Piat, Stéphane-Joseph. *The Story of a Family: The Home of St. Thérèse of Lisieux.* Translated by a Benedictine of Stanbrook Abbey. Rockford, IL: TAN Books, 1994.

Saint-Jure, Jean Baptiste and Saint Claude de la Columbière. *Trustful Surrender to Divine Providence: The Secret of Peace and Happiness.* Charlotte, NC: TAN Books, 2012.

Seewald, Peter. *Benedict XVI: An Intimate Portrait.* Translated by Henry Taylor and Anne Englund Nash. San Francisco: Ignatius Press, 2008.

Sheen, Fulton J. *Sheen's Guide to Contentment.* New York: Maco Publishing Co., 1967.

———. *The World's First Love.* New York: McGraw-Hill Book Co., 1952.

Sincardo, Joseph. *St. Rita of Cascia: Saint of the Impossible (Wife, Mother, Widow, Nun).* Charlotte, NC: TAN Books, 2011.

Solinas, Enrico. *Servo di Dio Vittorio Trancanelli. L'amore di Dio in sala operatoria e nella vita.* Milan, Italy: Elledici, 2013.

Thérèse of Lisieux. *St. Thérèse of Lisieux, Her Last Conversa-tions.* Washington D.C.: ICS Publications, 1977.

The Holy Bible: Revised Standard Version Catholic Edition. Char-lotte, NC: Saint Benedict Press, 2010.

Tolkien, J. R. R. *The Letters of J.R.R. Tolkien.* New York: Hough-ton Mifflin Company, 2000.

Troisi, Simone and Christiana Paccini. *Chiara Corbella Petrillo: A Witness to Joy.* Translated by Charlotte J. Fasi. Manchester, NH: Sophia Institute Press, 2015.

Weigel, George. *Witness to Hope: The Biography of Pope John Paul II*. New York, Cliff Street Books, 2001.

Zahn, Gordon C. *In Solitary Witness. The Life of and Death of Franz Jägerstätter*. New York: Holt, Rinehart, and Winston, 1964.